Appalachian Trail Guide to Massachusetts–Connecticut

D1615655

Appalachian Trail Guide to

Massachusetts–Connecticut

Sue Spring

Editor

TWELFTH EDITION

APPALACHIAN TRAIL
CONSERVANCY

Harpers Ferry

Cover photo: Sages Ravine, Connecticut; Timothy Cummings
Half-title page photo: Race Mountain, Connecticut; Bob Fletcher
Title-page photo: Jug End, Massachusetts; Bob Fletcher
Please see page 222 for additional photography credits.

Published by Appalachian Trail Conservancy
P.O. Box 807
Harpers Ferry, West Virginia 25425

ISBN 978-1-889386-67-6

Twelfth edition
Printed in the United States of America on recycled paper.

Contents

The Appalachian Trail

Welcome to America's best-known long-distance footpath, the Appalachian Trail. If you've never visited it before, you're in for a memorable time, and we hope this official guidebook will help you make the most of it. If you know the Trail, but not this part of it, we hope this book will help you discover new aspects of an experience that changes from state to state, mile to mile, and season to season.

Not long after the end of World War I, a Massachusetts regional planner named Benton MacKaye envisioned a footpath along the crests of the mountains from New England to the southern Appalachians. The work of scores of volunteers helped that dream become the Appalachian Trail, which extends more than 2,179 miles between Katahdin in central Maine

Mt. Greylock summit

and Springer Mountain in northern Georgia. Its terrain ranges from swamp-land to near-vertical rock scrambles that challenge the fittest wilderness trekker; its white "blazes" lead from small-town streets to remote mountain ridges days from the nearest road crossing.

The "A.T.," as it's called by hikers, is a linear trail that can be enjoyed in small pieces or large chunks. Hikers follow its blazes on round-trip day-hikes, on loop-hikes (where side trails connect with it and form a loop), on one-way "section-hikes" or overnight backpacking trips that cover short or long segments, or on end-to-end "thru-hikes" that cover the entire Trail. It is continuously marked, using a standard system of paint blazes and signs, and is cleared of undergrowth and maintained to permit single-file hiking. (Bicycles, horses, and motorized vehicles are not permitted along most of the route.) Many campsites and more than 250 primitive woodland shelters are located along the Trail, typically about a day's hike apart. The path itself is usually dirt, or rock, or grass, and only very short segments are paved or wheelchair-accessible.

This remarkable footpath is much more than just a walk through the woods. When it was first begun in the 1920s and completed in the 1930s, it was little-known and rarely traveled. Large parts of it were on private property. Since 1968, it has been a part of the same national park system that includes Yellowstone, Yosemite, and the Great Smoky Mountains. Its official name today is the Appalachian National Scenic Trail, and 99.6 percent of it runs over public lands. Hundreds of roads cross it, and scores of side trails intersect with it. In some parts, the Trail "corridor" is only a few hundred feet wide; in other parts, entire mountains are protected by it.

Unlike other well-known national parks, there's no "main entrance" to the A.T., with a gate and a ranger collecting tickets. You can begin or end your hike at hundreds of places between its northern and southern ends. As the longest, skinniest part of America's national park system, the A.T. stretches across fourteen different states and passes through more than sixty federal, state, and local parks and forests. Maybe the most important difference between the A.T. and other national-park units is that it was built by volunteers, and volunteers still are responsible for keeping it up. The A.T. relies on a system known as "cooperative man-agement" rather than on a large, paid federal staff. Yes, there are a handful of National Park Service staff members and a ranger assigned

Volunteer Trail maintainers

to the Appalachian Trail Park Office in Harpers Ferry, West Virginia, but thousands of the people who maintain, patrol, and monitor the footpath and its surrounding lands are outdoor lovers like you. Each year, as members of thirty maintaining clubs up and down the Appalachians, they annually volunteer almost two hundred thousand hours of their time looking after this public treasure. They would welcome your help.

About the Appalachian Trail Conservancy—We are the volunteer-based organization that teaches people about the Trail, coordinates the work of the maintaining clubs, and works with the government agencies, individuals, and companies that own the land that the Trail passes over. The membership of the Appalachian Trail Conservancy (ATC) includes hikers and Trail enthusiasts who elect a volunteer Board of Directors every two years. Members' dues and contributions help support a paid staff of about forty-five people at the ATC headquarters in Harpers Ferry; at regional offices in New England, Pennsylvania, Virginia, and North Carolina; and at a sales distribution center, also in West Virginia. Our Web site, <www.appalachiantrail.org>, is a good source of information about the Trail. Information about contacting the Conservancy is at the back of this book.

Maine Appalachian Trail Club—www.matc.org
Appalachian Mountain Club—www.outdoors.org
Dartmouth Outing Club—www.dartmouth.edu/~doc
Green Mountain Club—www.greenmountainclub.org
AMC Berkshire Chapter—www.amcberkshire.org
AMC Connecticut Chapter—www.ct-amc.org
New York–New Jersey Trail Conference—www.nynjtc.org
Wilmington Trail Club—www.wilmingtontrailclub.org
Batona Hiking Club—www.batonahikingclub.org
AMC Delaware Valley Chapter—www.amcdv.org
Philadelphia Trail Club—m.zanger.tripod.com
Blue Mountain Eagle Climbing Club—www.bmecc.org
Allentown Hiking Club—www.allentownhikingclub.org
Susquehanna Appalachian Trail Club—www.satc-hike.org
York Hiking Club—www.yorkhikingclub.com
Cumberland Valley A.T. Club—www.cvatclub.org
Mountain Club of Maryland—www.mcomd.org
Potomac Appalachian Trail Club—www.potomacappalachian.org
Old Dominion Appalachian Trail Club—www.odatc.org
Tidewater Appalachian Trail Club—www.tidewateratc.org
Natural Bridge Appalachian Trail Club—www.nbatc.org
Roanoke Appalachian Trail Club—www.ratc.org
Outdoor Club of Virginia Tech—www.outdoor.org.vt.edu
Piedmont Appalachian Trail Hikers—www.path-at.org
Mount Rogers Appalachian Trail Club—www.mratc.org
Tennessee Eastman Hiking Club—www.tehcc.org
Carolina Mountain Club—www.carolinamtnclub.com
Smoky Mountains Hiking Club—www.smhclub.org
Nantahala Hiking Club—www.maconcommunity.org/nhc
Georgia Appalachian Trail Club—www.georgia-atclub.org

Tips for enjoying the Appalachian Trail

Follow the blazes—The Appalachian Trail is marked for daylight travel in both directions, using a system of painted "blazes" on trees, posts, and rocks. There are some local variations, but most hikers grasp the system quickly. Above treeline, and where snow or fog may obscure paint marks, posts and rock piles called "cairns" are used to identify the route.

A blaze is a rectangle of paint in a prominent place along a trail. White-paint blazes two inches wide and six inches high mark the A.T. itself. Side trails and shelter trails use blue blazes; blazes of other colors and shapes mark other intersecting trails. Two white blazes, one above the other, signal an obscure turn, route change, incoming side trail, or other situation that requires you to be especially alert to changes in direction. In some states, one of the two blazes will be offset in the direction of the turn.

If you have gone a quarter-mile without seeing a blaze, stop. Retrace your steps until you locate a blaze. Then, check to ensure that you haven't missed a turn. Often a glance backward will reveal blazes meant for hikers traveling in the opposite direction.

Volunteer Trail maintainers regularly relocate small sections of the

White blaze

Double blaze

path around hazards or undesirable features or off private property. When your map or guidebook indicates one route, and the blazes show another, follow the blazes.

A few cautions—The A.T. is a scenic trail through the forests of the Appalachian Mountains. It is full of natural splendors and is fun to hike, and parts of it run near roads and across fairly level ground. But, most of the Trail is very steep and runs deep in the woods, along the crests of rocky mountain ridges, miles from the nearest houses or paved roads. It will test your physical conditioning and skills. Plan your hike, and prepare sensibly.

Before you set out to hike the Trail, take a few minutes to review the information in this guidebook. It is as current as possible, but conditions and footpath locations sometimes change in between guidebook editions. On the Trail, please pay close attention to—and follow—the blazes and any directional signs that mark the route, even if the book describes a different route.

Although we have included some basic tips for preparing for an A.T. hike in the back of this guidebook (see page 182), this is not a "how-to" guide to backpacking. Many good books of that sort are available in your local bookstore and library. If you've never hiked before, we recommend that you take the time to read one or two and to research equipment, camping techniques, and trip planning. If your only hiking and camping experience is in local parks and forests, be aware that hiking and

Post

Cairn

camping in the mountains can be extremely strenuous and disorienting and has its own particular challenges. You will sometimes encounter wildlife and will have to make do with primitive (or nonexistent) sanitary facilities. Remember that water in the backcountry, even at water sources mentioned in this guidebook, needs to be treated for microorganisms before you drink it.

Responsibility for safety—Finally, know that you are responsible for your own safety and for the safety of those with you and for making sure that your food and water are safe for consumption. Hiking the A.T. is no more dangerous than many other popular outdoor activities, but, although the Trail is part of the national park system, it is not the proverbial "walk in the park," and help may be some distance away. The Appalachian Trail Conservancy and its member clubs cannot ensure the safety of any hiker on the Trail. As a hiker, you assume the risk for any accident, illness, or injury that might occur there.

Leave No Trace—As more and more people use the Trail and other backcountry areas, it becomes more important to learn to enjoy wild places without ruining them. The best way to do this is to understand and practice the principles of Leave No Trace, (shown at right), a seven-point ethic for enjoying the backcountry that applies to everything from a picnic outing to a long-distance expedition. Leave No Trace, Inc., is a nonprofit organization dedicated to teaching the principles of low-impact use. For more information, contact Leave No Trace at <www.lnt.org>, or call (800) 332-4100.

Public transportation and shuttle services—Many sections of the Trail are served by persons providing shuttles to hikers, and some sections are reachable by public transportation. This is especially true for Massachusetts—see page 43. For the most up-to-date list of those services, please visit the Hike section of the ATC Web site, <www.appalachiantrail.org>, or call (304) 535-6331.

1. **Plan ahead and prepare**. Evaluate the risks associated with your outing, identify campsites and destinations in advance, use maps and guides, and be ready for bad weather. When people don't plan ahead, they're more likely to damage the backcountry.

2. **Travel and camp on durable surfaces.** Stay on trails and don't bushwhack short-cuts across switchbacks or other bends in the path. Keep off fragile trailside areas, such as bogs or alpine zones. Camp in designated spots, such as shelters and existing campsites, so that unspoiled areas aren't trampled and denuded.

3. **Dispose of waste properly.** Bury or pack out excrement, including pet droppings. Pack out all trash and food waste, including that left behind by others. Don't bury trash or food, and don't try to burn packaging materials in campfires.

4. **Leave what you find.** Don't take flowers or other sensitive natural resources. Don't disturb artifacts, such as native American arrowheads or the stone walls and cellar holes of historical woodland homesteads.

5. **Minimize campfire impacts.** Campfires are enjoyable, but they also create the worst visual and ecological impact of any backcountry camping practice. If possible, cook on a backpacking stove instead of a fire. Where fires are permitted, build them only in established fire rings, and don't add rocks to an existing ring. Keep fires small. Burn only dead and downed wood that can be broken by hand—leave axes and saws at home. Never leave your campfire unattended, and drown it when you leave.

6. **Respect wildlife.** Don't feed or disturb wildlife. Store food properly to avoid attracting bears, varmints, and rodents. If you bring a pet, keep it leashed.

7. **Be considerate of other visitors.** Limit overnight groups to ten or fewer, twenty-five on day trips. Minimize noise and intrusive behavior, including cell phone use around others. Share shelters and other facilities. Be considerate of Trail neighbors.

How to use this book

We suggest that you use this book in conjunction with the waterproof Trail maps that were sold with it. Information about services available in towns near the Trail is updated annually in the *Appalachian Trail Thru-Hikers' Companion*. Mileage and shelter information for the entire Trail is updated annually in the *Appalachian Trail Data Book*.

Although the Trail is usually well marked and experienced hikers may be able to follow it without either guidebook or map, using the book and the maps will not only help you keep from getting lost or disoriented, but will also help you get more out of your hike.

Before you start your hike:

■ *Decide where you want to go and which Trail features you hope to see.* Use the book to help you plan your trip. The chapter on loop hikes (page 168) lists a number of popular day-hikes and short trips that have proven popular with hikers along this part of the Trail. The introductions to each section give more detail, summarizing scenic and cultural highlights along the route that you may wish to visit.

■ *Calculate mileage for linear or loop hikes.* Each chapter lists mileage between landmarks on the route, along with details to help you follow the path. Use the mileage and descriptions to determine how far you must hike, how long it will take you, and where you can camp if you're taking an overnight or long-distance hike.

■ *Find the Trail.* Use the section maps included in the guidebook to locate parking areas near the A.T. and the "Trailheads" or road crossings where the footpath crosses the highway. In some cases, the guidebook includes directions to nearby towns and commercial areas where you can find food, supplies, and lodging.

After you begin hiking:

- *Identify landmarks.* Deduce where you are along the Trail by comparing the descriptions in the guidebook and the features on the waterproof maps to the landscape you're hiking through. Much of the time, the Trail's blazes will lead you through seemingly featureless woodlands, where the only thing you can see in most directions is trees, but you will be able to check your progress periodically at viewpoints, meadows, mountain tops, stream crossings, road crossings, and Trailside structures.

- *Learn about the route.* Native Americans, colonial-era settlers, Civil War soldiers, nineteenth-century farmers, pioneering railroaders, and early industrial entrepreneurs explored these hills long before the A.T. was built. Although much of what they left behind has long since been overgrown and abandoned, your guidebook will point out old settlements and forest roads and put the landscape in its historical context. It will touch on the geology, natural history, and modern-day ecosystems of the eastern mountains.

- *Find campsites and side trails.* The guidebook includes directions to other trails, as well as creeks, mountain springs, and established tenting and shelter sites.

Areas covered

Each of the eleven official Appalachian Trail guidebooks describes several hundred miles of the Trail. In some cases, that includes a single state, such as Maine or Pennsylvania. In other cases, the guidebook may include several states, such as the one covering northern Virginia, West Virginia, and Maryland. Because so much of the Trail is in Virginia (more than 500 miles of it), a hiker needs to use four different guidebooks to cover that entire state.

The eleven guidebooks are:

Maine
New Hampshire–Vermont
Massachusetts–Connecticut

New York–New Jersey
Pennsylvania
Maryland and Northern Virginia
Shenandoah National Park
Central Virginia
Southwest Virginia
Tennessee–North Carolina
North Carolina–Georgia

How the guidebook is divided

Rather than trying to keep track of several hundred miles of the Trail from beginning to end, the Trail's maintainers break it down into smaller "sections." Each section covers the area between important road crossings or natural features and can vary from three to thirty miles in length. A typical section is from five to fifteen miles long. This guidebook is organized according to those sections, beginning with the northernmost in the coverage area and ending with the southernmost. Each section makes up a chapter. A summary of distances for the entire guidebook appears near the end of the book.

How sections are organized

Brief description of section—Each section begins with a brief description of the route. The description mentions highlights and prominent features and gives a sense of what it's like to hike the section as a whole.

Section map—The map shows how to find the Trail from your vehicle (it is not a detailed map and should not be relied on for navigating the Trail) and includes notable roads along with a rough depiction of the Trail route, showing shelter locations.

Shelters and campsites—Each chapter also includes an overview of shelters and campsites for the section, including the distances between shelters and information about water supplies. Along some parts of the Trail, particularly north of the Mason-Dixon Line, the designated sites are the only areas in which camping is permitted. In other parts of the

Trail, even where "dispersed camping" is allowed, we recommend that hikers "Leave No Trace" (see page 9) and reduce their impact on the Trail's resources by using established campsites. If camping is restricted in a section, it will be noted here.

Trail description—Trail descriptions appear on the right-hand pages of each chapter. Although the description reads from north to south, it is organized for both northbound and southbound hikers. Northbound hikers should start at the end of the chapter and read up, using the mileages in the right-hand column. Southbound hikers should read down, using the mileages in the left-hand column. The description includes obvious landmarks you will pass, although it may not include all stream crossings, summits, or side trails. Where the Trail route becomes confusing, the guide will provide both north- and southbound directions from the landmark. When a feature appears in **bold** type, it means that you should see the section highlights for more detail.

Section highlights—On the left-hand pages of each chapter, you will find cultural, historical, natural, and practical information about the **bold**

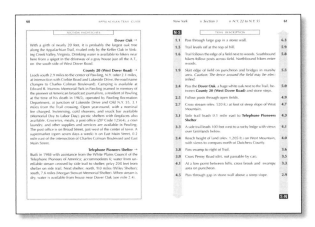

items in the Trail description. That includes detailed information about Trailheads, shelters, and campsites, along with notes on the historical and cultural resources of the route, notes on landforms and natural history, and descriptions of side trails.

End of section—The northern and southern ends of each section are noted in **bold** in the Trail description and detailed in the section highlights at the beginning and ending of each chapter of the book, respectively. The information includes brief directions about how to find the Trailhead from the highway; information about where to park, if parking is available; distances to nearby towns and facilities; and notes on the services available near the Trail, such as grocery stores and restaurants.

Guidebook conventions

North or "compass-north"?—For the sake of convenience, the directions *north, south, east* and *west* in the guide refer to the general north–south orientation of the Trail, rather than the true north or magnetic north of maps and charts. In other words, when a hiker is northbound on the Trail, whatever is to his left will be referred to as "west" and whatever is to the right will be "east." For southbounders, the opposite is true.

Although this is instinctively the way A.T. hikers orient themselves, it can be slightly confusing for the first-time A.T. hiker, since the Trail does not always follow an actual north–south orientation. For example, you might be "northbound" along the Trail (headed toward Maine), but, because of a sharp turn or a switchback up the side of a mountain, your compass will tell you you're actually pointed south for a while. Nevertheless, in this guide, a trail or road intersecting on the left side of the A.T. for the northbound hiker will always be referred to as "intersecting on the west side of the A.T.," even where the compass says otherwise.

When the compass direction of an object is important, as when directing attention to a certain feature seen from a viewpoint, the guidebook will refer to "compass-north," "compass-west," and so forth.

Undocumented features—The separate waterproof hiking maps meant to accompany this guide generally reflect all the landmarks discussed here. Because the maps are extremely detailed, some features that appear on them, such as streams and old woods roads, may not be mentioned in the guidebook if they are not important landmarks. Other side trails that the hiker encounters may not be mentioned or mapped at all; in general, this is because the unmarked trails lead onto private property, and Trail managers wish to discourage their use.

Using the Trail in Massachusetts and Connecticut

The 142 miles of the Appalachian Trail in Massachusetts and Connecticut, ideal for day-hikes and weekend backpacking, offer an array of landscapes—skirting riverbanks and the outskirts of classic Berskshire towns as it crosses valleys to peaks and outcrops overlooking those bucolic settings but also slipping placidly into the wooded "green tunnels" so often associated with the A.T.

Two chapters of the Appalachian Mountain Club maintain the footpath and facilities and manage the surrounding lands in cooperation with ATC and federal and state agency partners.

In Massachusetts, the responsibility for maintaining the Trail was originally divided among three groups. The Berkshire Chapter of the Appalachian Mountain Club took care of the Trail from the Sages Ravine brook crossing to Tyringham; the Metawampe Club (outdoor club of the University of Massachusetts faculty), from Tyringham to Washington; and the Mt. Greylock Ski Club, from Washington to the Vermont–Massachusetts state line. In 1979, maintenance responsibilities for the Appalachian Trail in Massachusetts were assigned to the Berkshire Chapter. A new committee, the Berkshire Chapter Appalachian Trail Committee, in partnership with ATC, the National Park Service, and what is now the Massachusetts Department of Conservation and Recreation, Division of Forests and Parks, was organized to take responsibility for Trail maintenance and land management. The Trail is divided into ten hiking sections and twenty-seven maintenance sections, with a maintainer for each section. Work parties organized by the committee and the Division of Forests and Parks ridgerunners have tackled larger construction and maintenance projects since 1980 while also giving other members an opportunity to participate. Each summer, AMC and the state of Massachusetts hire ridgerunners to patrol the Trail and provide information and advice to hikers.

After passage of the Massachusetts Appalachian Trail Act in 1969, the state Department of Natural Resources (now the Department of Conservation and Recreation) proceeded to acquire land to protect the Trail. The Division of Forests and Parks and its regional supervisor made an in-depth study of the Trail location, land titles, and landowners' attitudes and their willingness to make a conveyance to the state. The department also published a comprehensive study of the Trail. Where locations of the A.T. were unsatisfactory, the regional supervisor, after consulting with area Trail clubs, began relocating it. Those initial efforts by the commonwealth slowed because of a lack of funds. After federal passage of 1978 amendments to the National Trails System Act, funding became available, and the state and the National Park Service (NPS) worked together to finish the acquisition. By May 2008, all the footpath had been protected in the state, while two tracts of about 345 acres in buffer lands remained to be acquired by the NPS.

The Trail along the Housatonic River in Connecticut has been maintained by the Connecticut Chapter of the Appalachian Mountain Club (AMC) since 1949. From 1949 until 1979, twenty-three miles east of the river were maintained by Seymour Smith of Watertown, who gave extraordinary service to the Appalachian Trail. His former section is now part of the Connecticut Blue Trail System. The Trail is divided into nineteen sections for purposes of maintenance, with one or two individuals responsible for each section, all under the direction of the Trails Committee of the Connecticut Chapter.

In 1978, the Connecticut Appalachian Trail Committee was formed to help guide the National Park Service in its efforts to permanently protect the Trail. This committee was composed of representatives of organizations concerned with the Trail, including the ATC, AMC, Department of Environmental Protection, Housatonic Valley Association, Connecticut Forest and Park Association, and The Nature Conservancy. In 1979, representatives from Trail towns were added. A subcommittee was formed in February 1979, as a direct result of pressure from landowners. This subcommittee, known as the Connecticut Appalachian Trail Management Advisory Committee, published the Connecticut Appalachian Trail Management Plan. (This management plan has since been revised by the Trails Committee of the Connecticut Chapter of AMC.) The committee met regularly until December 1980, when the preferred route of the Trail was established on paper (although many parts had not been actually acquired). The committee then ceased to function. By May 2008, 0.7 mile of the footpath in Connecticut remained to be protected through the acquisition of two tracts totalling 127 acres.

A paid ridgerunner program has been in effect since 1979, and a volunteer guide program since 1980. In 1984, the AMC began hiring a seasonal caretaker to work at Sages Ravine, which is basically the boundary line of the two states.

To assist the volunteers in both states and manage other club activities in the area, AMC maintains a southern New England office within ATC's Kellogg Conservation Center in South Egremont, Mass.; (413) 528-8003. Founded in 1876 and the oldest nonprofit conservation and recreational organization in the United States, the AMC promotes the protection, enjoyment, and wise use of the mountains, rivers, and trails of the Northeast. Through its more than 75,000 members and with regional chapters from Maine to Washington, D.C., the AMC supports the belief that the mountains and rivers have an intrinsic worth and also provide recreational opportunity, spiritual renewal, and ecological and economic health for the region. AMC encourages people to enjoy the natural world because it believes that successful conservation depends on this experience. In 1925, AMC leaders helped Benton MacKaye form the Appalachian Trail Conference (now Conservancy). The club publishes maps, guidebooks, and the periodical *Appalachia* and has supported many efforts to research, preserve, and conserve the natural mountain landscape in the northeastern United States. AMC manages an extensive system of shelters, trails, and mountain huts in the Northeast.

For more information on the club, write AMC, 5 Joy Street, Boston, Mass. 02108, call (617) 523-0636, or visit <www.outdoors.org>.

Appalachian Trail Conservancy
Regional office—South Egremont, Mass., (413) 528-8002
National office—Harpers Ferry, W.Va., (304) 535-6331
<www.appalachiantrail.org>
<incident@appalachiantrail.org>

National Park Service
Appalachian Trail Park Office—Harpers Ferry, W.Va., (304) 535-6278
<www.nps.gov/appa>

Massachusetts
Dial 911; if 911 is not available, dial the following local numbers:
State Police—Cheshire, (413) 743-4700; Lee, (413) 243-0600
Berkshire County Emergency Dispatch—(413) 442-0512
Mt. Greylock State Reservation—(413) 499-4263

Connecticut
Dial 911; if 911 is not available, dial the following local numbers:
State Police—northern areas, (860) 824-2500; Kent, (860) 567-6800
Litchfield County Dispatch—(860) 567-3877
Department of Environmental Protection—(860) 424-3333

Guidelines for Trail Users

- Stay on the Trail. Respect landowner privacy; approach private homes only in an emergency. Especially in Connecticut, the Trail corridor is narrower than it may seem on maps.
- Camp only at designated campsites. Leave the area cleaner than you found it.
- Please use the bear boxes, where available, to store your food overnight, to help local volunteers in their efforts to prevent bears from becoming a nuisance. Bear boxes at this writing are placed at all Massachusetts overnight sites except Mt. Wilcox North and Mark Noepel shelters, at Limestone Spring Shelter, and at Paradise Lane and Sage Ravine campsites. If a bear box is not available, it is essential that you properly hang your food (see page 187).
- Park only in designated areas.
- Please use small backpacking stoves. In Massachusetts, fires are permitted in state-built fireplaces only and are prohibited at Upper Goose Pond, Laurel Ridge Campsite, and Sages Ravine. **Fires are not permitted in any season on the A.T. in Connecticut.**
- Hikers should use privies at all campsites and shelters. Some privies are of the mouldering variety and actively compost human waste; please read and follow instructions for use. Elsewhere, human waste should be disposed of at least 50 feet from the Trail and 200 feet from water. Dig a shallow hole and, after use, replace the ground cover.
- Travel in groups smaller than 12.
- State and federal laws prohibit vehicles, mountain bikes, and horses from the Trail.
- Control your pet at all times.
- Leave flowers, plants, and wildlife for the enjoyment of others.
- Designated campsites and shelters are provided for one-night-use only; two nights are permitted in cases of bad weather or illness. Shelters are not for group use.
- **Group areas and sites are for group use only.** "Group" is defined as a party of more than five members affiliated with an organization, agency, or commercial operation.

- Keep the A.T. and Trailheads free of litter. Carry home what you carried in.
- When washing yourself or your dishes, never contaminate the water source. Treat all unprotected drinking water. In Connecticut, please use the wash pits provided at all the designated sites as the sole washing area for dishes, for brushing teeth, and other "gray water" uses. Pack out all food scraps collected on the wash pit screens.

Hiking During Hunting Season—Hunting is allowed along many parts of the A.T. Though prohibited in many state parks and on National Park Service lands—whether acquired specifically for protection of the Appalachian Trail or as part of another unit of the national park system—most of the boundary lines that identify these lands are not always obvious. It may be very difficult for hunters to know that they are on Park Service lands. Hunters who approach the A.T. from the side, and who do not know that they are on Trail lands, also may have no idea that the Trail is nearby. The Trail traverses lands of several other types of ownership, including state gamelands, on which hunting is allowed.

About 50 percent of the Trail in Massachusetts is open to hunting.

Some hunting areas are marked by permanent or temporary signs, but any sign is subject to vandalism and removal. The prudent hiker, especially in the fall, makes himself aware of local hunting seasons. Deer season, typically in the months of October, November, December, and January, should be a time for special caution by hikers.

Hikers should call ATC or check state Web sites or ATC's site, <www. appalachiantrail.org>, for detailed information about hunting seasons. ATC recommends that hikers wear plenty of highly visible "blaze orange" clothing when hunters are sharing the woods.

Trail Section	Miles from Vermont Line	Miles from New York Line	Site
Mass. 1	2.3	139.7	Sherman Brook Primitive Campsite
Mass. 2	7.1	134.9	Wilbur Clearing Shelter side trail
Mass. 2	13.7	128.3	Mark Noepel Shelter side trail
Mass. 3	22.7	119.3	Crystal Mountain Campsite side trail
Mass. 4	30.4	111.6	Kay Wood Shelter side trail
Mass. 5	39.2	102.8	October Mountain Shelter side trail
Mass. 6	48.0	94.0	Upper Goose Pond Cabin side trail
Mass. 7	58.1	83.9	Shaker Campsite side trail
Mass. 7	62.2	79.8	Mt. Wilcox North Shelter side trail
Mass. 7	64.0	78.0	Mt. Wilcox South Shelter side trail
Mass. 8	69.3	72.7	Tom Leonard Shelter side trail
Mass. 10	83.6	58.4	Glen Brook Shelter
Mass. 10	83.7	58.3	Hemlocks Shelter
Mass. 10	85.5	56.5	Race Brook Falls Trail
Mass. 10	88.5	53.5	Laurel Ridge Campsite

Trail Section	Miles from Vermont Line	Miles from New York Line	Site
Conn. 1	90.3	51.7	Sages Ravine Brook Campsite
Conn. 1	92.5	49.5	Brassie Brook Shelter
Conn. 1	93.1	48.9	Ball Brook Campsite
Conn. 1	93.7	48.3	Riga Shelter
Conn. 2	101.2	40.8	Limestone Spring Shelter side trail
Conn. 3	108.3	33.7	Belter's Campsite
Conn. 3	111.1	30.9	Sharon Mountain Campsite
Conn. 3	113.5	28.5	Pine Swamp Brook Shelter side trail
Conn. 3	116.9	25.1	Caesar Brook Campsite
Conn. 4	120.3	21.7	Silver Hill Campsite
Conn. 4	123.1	18.9	Stony Brook Campsite
Conn. 4	123.5	18.5	Stewart Hollow Brook Shelter
Conn. 5	130.8	11.2	Mt. Algo Shelter side trail
Conn. 5	133.7	8.3	Schaghticoke Mountain Campsite side trail
Conn. 5	139.2	2.8	Ten Mile River Shelter side trail

A walk south along the A.T. through Massachusetts and Connecticut

The Appalachian Trail in Massachusetts, from where it enters the state, at the Long Trail terminus at the southern end of the Green Mountains on the Vermont border, to where it leaves, at Sages Ravine near the Connecticut line, is situated entirely in Berkshire County.

South of Mt. Greylock, the route travels across much of the Berkshire Highlands (also called the southern Hoosac Range). It is generally level and swampy once you climb out of the valleys, and, when the leaves are on the trees, you may not even be aware that you're following a mountain trail. The Trail also passes through some very isolated areas, however, so take proper precautions. In general, the terrain is dominated by two rivers—the Hoosic and the Housatonic—and three mountain ranges—the Greylock Range, the Berkshire Highlands, and the Taconic Range.

Beginning in the north, the Trail enters Massachusetts from Vermont four miles north of Mass. 2 in North Adams and descends into the Hoosac Valley, carved out by the Hoosic River, a tributary of the Hudson. It passes through the outskirts of North Adams, then ascends the first of the three ranges, the Greylock massif, south over Prospect Mountain Ridge, Mt. Williams, and Mt. Fitch to Mt. Greylock itself, the state's most famous mountain. From the southern end of Greylock, on Saddle Ball Mountain, the A.T. bears east, back into the valley of the Hoosic River, and through the small town of Cheshire.

From Cheshire, it climbs into the Berkshire Highlands, the second of the three ranges, descending again in the small town of Dalton at the headwaters of the Housatonic River (the Housatonic flows into Long Island Sound). From Dalton, the A.T. climbs into the Berkshires again, crossing Pittsfield Road, traversing Bald Top, passing Finerty Pond in October Mountain State Forest, and crossing U.S. 20 (Jacob's Ladder Highway) and the Massachusetts Turnpike (Interstate 90) at Greenwater Pond. Beyond that, it ascends to a scenic ridge above Upper Goose Pond, a spectacular glacial lake, descends into beautiful Tyringham Valley, formed by a tributary of the Housatonic, then climbs again into Beartown State Forest, where it skirts Benedict Pond. Continuing southwest, the Trail enters

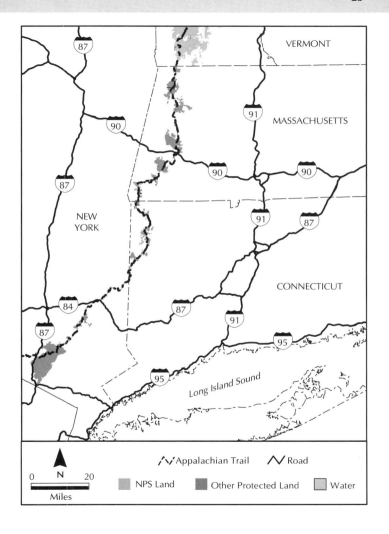

VERMONT

MASSACHUSETTS

NEW
YORK

CONNECTICUT

Long Island Sound

0   N   20
Miles

/\/ Appalachian Trail   /\/ Road

NPS Land   Other Protected Land   Water

East Mountain State Forest, crossing over Warner and June mountains, then descends to the Housatonic River again, where it reaches U.S. 7 in the valley, near the site of the last gasp of Shays' Rebellion and ATC's Kellogg Conservation Center.

After crossing the Housatonic Valley a final time, it climbs the third major range of mountains, the rocky and difficult Taconics, at Jug End Mountain. From there, it turns south along peaks of the Taconic Plateau to Mt. Everett, then crosses Mt. Race and descends to Sages Ravine, just north of the Massachusetts–Connecticut state line.

From Sages Ravine, near the Massachusetts–Connecticut line, the Trail leads south over Bear Mountain, the highest summit in Connecticut. It then crosses Lions Head, at the southern end of the Taconic Range, descends to the valley floor near Salisbury, and bears southeast to cross the Housatonic River at Falls Village. Soon crossing the river again, the Trail traverses the Housatonic State Forest and Sharon Mountain, reaching the Housatonic River again at Cornwall Bridge. For about five miles, the route follows the west bank of the river, then passes over St. Johns Ledges and Caleb's Peak just west of Kent. The Trail takes a southerly route over Algo and Schaghticoke mountains, crossing into New York and back into Connecticut on the shoulder of Schaghticoke. It crosses the Ten Mile River and reenters New York at Hoyt Road near Sherman, Connecticut.

The northern portion of the Trail passes near Salisbury, which became known as the "arsenal of the Revolution" and was the source of some of the highest-quality iron ore in the world for almost two hundred years. One of the more famous blast furnaces, built after that war, was located at South Pond, west of Lions Head. It produced all types of iron implements and weapons, and legend has it that one of the anchors for the U.S.S. Constitution ("Old Ironsides") was forged there. The ore was brought uphill from the mine on the present Lakeville-to-Millerton Road, and the finished product was hauled downhill to the Hudson River.

South of Salisbury, the Trail passes the "Great Falls" near Falls Village on the Housatonic River. Just north of the dam lie foundations of the famous Ames Iron Works, a factory founded in 1833 that employed as many as 800 men in three shifts and produced cannons for the Civil War made from Salisbury iron. Ames' "super cannon" put the company into bankruptcy when its contract with the Union Army was cancelled at the end of the war. Later, railroad car wheels were manufactured at this site. As you hike by the falls, you will pass the ruins of a blast furnace that was still operating into the middle of the nineteenth century.

The name *Housatonic* comes from the Mohican Indian word for "place beyond the mountain." It was first explored by Europeans in 1614. Rising near Pittsfield, Massachusetts, it flows southward 148 miles through Connecticut to Long Island Sound. Historically, the river's power made this an important industrial area. It drops 959 feet in its first 119 miles, which makes it popular for canoeing and kayaking between Falls Village and Cornwall Bridge and a source of hydro power farther to the south. Pollution has been a problem, however, particularly near Pittsfield, where PCB contamination led to a site being added to the federal Environmental Protection Agency's "Superfund" list; the pollution there is still being mitigated. Today, the water is relatively clean, but fishing is on a "catch-and-release" basis, and the river should not be used by hikers as a source of drinking water.

Near Kent, the Trail crosses property long owned by the Stanley Works of New Britain, then very briefly through the lands of the Schaghticoke Tribal Nation, the only Indian reservation along the entire A.T. This was the last major Indian stronghold in the state, and remnants of prehistoric native-American encampments date to more than 4,000 years ago. In 1730, about 100 Indian families—what was left of several tribes decimated by colonial wars—lived at the "divided-broad-river-place" south of Kent. Two decades later, only 18 remained. Today, about half a dozen families live there. Aside from the Schaghticoke state reservation and the protected lands through which the A.T. passes, the area's scenic beauty and proximity to New York makes its real estate some of the state's most coveted.

The natural setting of Massachusetts and Connecticut

Although the Trail through western Massachusetts and Connecticut is particularly favored—despite the sense of remoteness on the footpath itself—for its proximity to several classic New England towns and its remnants of colonial America, its natural setting, now a century removed from most timbering and other extractions, underscores a sense of place all its own.

Wildlife

By René Laubach, Berkshire Sanctuaries
Massachusetts Audubon Society

The Appalachian Trail in Massachusetts and Connecticut passes through the northern hardwood forest, a large, rather homogeneous plant community interspersed with meadows, wetlands, streams, cultivated land, and settled areas. Each natural community within the larger hardwood forest system has its own characteristic wildlife—birds, reptiles, amphibians, and mammals.

Birds

The forested uplands are home to many species of breeding birds. The lush foliage of late spring and summer often conceals even the gaudiest singers, so that some familiarity with the songs of the more common species can greatly enhance your appreciation of birds.

Most birds sing to advertise ownership of territory during the breeding season of late spring and early summer. Most forest species rely upon loud song to make their presence known. Among the more omnipresent songsters is the ovenbird (actually a warbler); its loud, ringing, "teacher, teacher, teacher" refrain is very common. Winter wrens, tiny brown birds with short, erect tails, scamper mouse-like through the underbrush, but sing a very long, babbling, and musical song from an elevated perch. The song of the white-throated sparrow, often written as "old Sam Peabody, Peabody, Peabody," has a beautiful, clear, plaintive quality.

Perhaps the best singers of all are two members of the thrush family. The flutelike tones of the hermit thrush are often heard in the early morning and early evening. A glimpse of this seven-inch-long bird may reveal a reddish-brown tail that the bird raises and slowly lowers. The wood thrush is a slightly larger species, heavily spotted below with black and sporting a reddish-brown head. Its "e-o-lay" phrases, interspersed throughout its beautiful, melodic music, are distinctive.

Two other thrushes also may be heard. The veery sings a flutelike "veer, veer, veer, veer" in down-the-scale fashion. At higher elevations (3,000 feet and above), the song of the Swainson's thrush may be heard.

Among the small, brightly colored wood warblers, perhaps 15 species are common to these forest habitats.

Stands of coniferous trees provide nesting habitat for the Blackburnian warbler (which sports a flame-orange head and breast) and numerous yellow-rumped warblers (myrtle).

Deciduous and mixed woods of broadleaf and needleleaf trees are home to the black-throated blue warbler, black-throated green warbler, black-and-white warbler (often seen creeping along trunks and branches in nuthatch-like fashion), and the American redstart. The redstart is black, orange, and white and often fans its tail as it searches for insect larvae among the foliage and branches. You also may see it fly-catching.

Hemlock stands near water are good places to find the beautiful Canada warbler, which bears a black necklace across its bright yellow breast. Two closely related species of water thrush, actually ground-dwelling warblers, are found near water: The northern frequents swamps, whereas the Louisiana is found near woodland brooks. Both species are spotted below and walk with characteristic bobbing motions (not to be confused with the larger spotted sandpiper).

Areas overgrown with raspberry, blackberry, and tree saplings (especially on slopes) are the haunts of the mourning warbler, a yellowish bird with a grayish hood. The breast has an almost black-flecked-crepe appearance, hence the common name.

Along shrubby streams, wet meadows, and similar habitats, the hiker is likely to encounter the yellow warbler and black-masked (male) common yellowthroat.

Second-growth woods and edges contain the colorful chestnut-sided warbler. Along with chestnut sides, the birds boast a bright-yellow crown and bright-white underparts.

Among the larger forest-canopy dwellers are the scarlet tanager (the male is bright scarlet with black wings and tail); rose-breasted grosbeak; and, in more open forest, black-headed, bright-orange northern (Baltimore) oriole. Also at home in woodland foliage are vireos, which are olive-green. Slightly larger than warblers, and much more deliberate in their movements, they usually are more difficult to locate visually than warblers. The most common vireo in deciduous forests is the red-eyed vireo, which sings almost incessantly in summer, even during the hottest portion of the day. Two other common species are the solitary vireo, which has a grayish head with white spectacles, and the yellow-throated vireo, which is more colorful, sporting yellow throat, breast, and spectacles.

Woodpeckers excavate for insects in dead and dying wood. They also drum loudly on dead wood to proclaim territory. The pileated is the largest species in the forest, almost as large as the crow. Its bright red crest is unmistakable. In flight, the white and black wings are distinctive. Usually, the hiker will see only the long, deep, rectangular excavations the bird has made in its search for carpenter ants, a favorite food. The colorful yellow-bellied sapsucker dines on sap and on the insects attracted to the sap that runs from the wells the bird bores. These quarter-inch-diameter holes are drilled in grids on birch, hemlock, and other species.

Among the larger woodland birds likely to be encountered is the ruffed grouse. This chicken-like bird may be seen eating high in a tree or on the woodland floor, where it flushes in a loud explosion of wings at one's approach. In spring and summer, males are often heard "drumming," a sound not unlike that of a small motor starting up and sputtering out.

The large terrestrial bird of the area (and one that has expanded its range, partially with the help of restocking programs) is the wild turkey. Consider yourself fortunate if you catch a glimpse of this wary bird.

Several species of raptorial birds frequent the area. The crow-sized broadwinged hawk has a banded black-and-white tail, as does the larger red-shouldered hawk. The latter is much less common than it once was. It is partial to wet habitats, often preying on reptiles and amphibians. Perhaps the best-known hawk is the red-tailed, a large hawk of semiopen country. The uniformly rusty tail of the adult bird is its best field mark. The groshawk is a large, long-tailed gray hawk of the northern forests that preys on birds. It is a year-round resident. Cooper's and sharp-shinned hawks are smaller relatives of groshawks and can sometimes be seen in swift pursuit of birds of prey or gliding rapidly above the tree tops. All three species have long tails and relatively short wings.

Owls are fairly common but seldom-seen nocturnal forest dwellers. The largest is the great horned owl, which has ear tufts and yellow eyes. It is large enough to tackle prey the size of grouse, rabbits, and skunks. The barred owl lacks ear tufts and has dark eyes. The barred prefers wet habitats. Its call is a distinctive, "Who cooks for you, who cooks for you all?"

Amphibians and Reptiles

Forests and wetlands alike are home to a variety of reptiles and amphibians, some extremely abundant, most overlooked. The tailed amphibians include salamanders, a species that has its greatest diversity in the southern Appalachians. In Massachusetts and Connecticut, a handful of species may be encountered. The most obvious is the red eft (the land-dwelling stage of the red-spotted newt). Red efts are bright reddish-orange (to warn potential predators that they are poisonous) and about 2¼ inches long. Dozens may be encountered on woodland trails, especially during wet weather. This attractive and interesting animal hatches from an egg laid in water, then spends two to three years on land before maturing and returning to lakes and ponds as a yellowish-green aquatic salamander.

The most abundant vertebrate animal in northeastern forests, although seldom seen, is the red-backed salamander. It is a slender, grayish creature with a reddish (or sometimes grayish) back. These animals spend the daylight hours beneath logs in the forest.

Two other woodland salamanders are quite common in number, yet seldom seen, except during their early-spring migrations to breeding ponds, called vernal pools. The spotted salamander is black with large, bright-yellow spots and six or eight inches long. The Jefferson's salamander, almost as large, is dark-gray with very small, bluish flecks. Both species emerge from underground during the first spring rains, when temperatures hover around 40 degrees Fahrenheit, to seek out ephemeral woodland ponds for breeding. Vernal pools are the only place where those species, wood frogs, and fairy shrimp can successfully breed.

Six common species of tailless amphibians (frogs and toads) inhabit this region. The woodland frog is two to three inches long and light brown, with a black "mask." It requires a vernal pool habitat for breeding but can be found on the woodland floor far from water. Its duck-like quacking can be heard at vernal pools on spring evenings.

The male of this area's smallest frog, the one-inch-long spring peeper, masses in swamp and marsh choruses to produce a loud, high-pitched "pee-ep" that sounds like sleigh bells. The tiny frogs are light brown and have a brown "X" on their backs. They cling to swamp vegetation with rough toe-tip pads and are seldom seen.

In summer, the voice of the largest and most aquatic member of the frog clan, the bullfrog, can be heard near still waters. The loud, resonant "jig-o-rum" of this species is a familiar summer sound along ponds and slow-moving rivers, where the larger males stake out territories.

Two other frogs that look a good deal alike, pickerel frog and leopard frog, can be found in area wetlands or in wet fields. Both are greenish-brown and have spots on their upper surface, but pickerel frogs' spots are square while leopard frogs' are oval.

The American toad, with its brown, warty skin, is a common inhabitant of the wetlands. It may grow to three inches in length. Toads, too, form breeding choruses in the spring.

The area's most often-seen reptiles are turtles. Two species are common. Eastern painted turtles usually are observed while basking on logs in ponds and along rivers. Its name refers to the red coloring of its underside. Its dark-green, low-domed shell is somewhat shiny and six to eight inches long. The much larger snapping turtle can grow to two feet and has a rough, often algae-covered shell. It is the top predator in many ponds and may be mistaken for a floating log. On land, this species is rather sluggish and, although menacing, hardly the danger to humans that some believe.

The wood turtle has a sculpted shell approximately seven inches long and can be found in fields or woodlands. Wood turtles hibernate during winter on the bottom of streams. In Massachusetts, they are a protected "species of special concern." The bog turtle and the spotted turtle (named for its yellow spots) are endangered. If you find either of these species, please report the location to state wildlife officials.

The most common snake in this area is the eastern garter snake. Brownish with yellow stripes, garter snakes are generally 1½ to 2 feet long and are often found in moist habitats. They feed on frogs, toads, and insects.

Three other fairly common, but much less observed snakes are the red-bellied snake, the ring-necked snake, and the DeKay's (or brown earth) snake. All are small, usually a foot or less in length, and tend to remain hidden under logs during daylight hours.

Only one snake in the area is poisonous, the endangered eastern timber rattlesnake. This magnificent snake is a local species that can be found on rocky hillsides, where it preys on rodents. Although rattlesnakes should not be taken lightly, their danger to humans has been greatly exaggerated. If you are fortunate enough to see one, watch it from a safe distance and do not harm it. (Dens are often encountered on the trek across Schagticoke Mountain near the Indian reservation.)

Mammals

Most mammals are nocturnal or crepuscular (active at dawn and dusk). The hiker who is on the Trail at those times will see a greater variety of mammal life. Among the familiar daytime mammals are the squirrels: red squirrel (in mixed and coniferous forests), eastern gray squirrel (in deciduous woods), and woodchuck or groundhog (a large plump squirrel of the woodland edge).

Common, yet not likely to be seen, are the strictly nocturnal flying squirrels. Two species—the northern, which inhabits higher, more northern areas, and the southern, preferring lower, more southern climes—are found in this region.

The eastern chipmunk is a small, striped ground squirrel, often first noticed after it gives its loud "clucking" or "chirping" alarm calls.

Cottontail rabbits, both eastern and New England, are found at the edges of woodlands, especially early and late in the day. The much larger snowshoe hare has been reintroduced in some of the higher areas. This mammal is aptly named, for its large hind feet give it excellent traction in deep snow, when its fur matches the color of the landscape.

Many other species of mammals, such as the raccoon, are common but, because of their habits, are seldom encountered. Tracks and scat (feces) are usually the best clues to their presence.

Two species of fox are quite common. The gray fox inhabits forests, where it climbs trees. It is slightly smaller than the red fox, which inhabits more open country. Both leave small doglike tracks in mud or snow. Fox tracks, however, tend to be in a straight line, unlike a dog's more randomly arranged pattern.

Foxes feed largely upon rodents: white-footed and deer mice (nocturnal); woodland and meadow jumping mice that can cover six inches in a bound; meadow voles, large, dark brown, prolific mice; and red-backed mice, common in coniferous and mixed woods.

Foxes and other predators often kill the tiny and abundant shrews found in the forest but seldom eat these insectivorous mammals, due to their disagreeable odors. Two common species in this area are the lead-gray short-tailed shrew (at four inches, the largest species) and the tiny, long-tailed masked shrew. Shrews are among the world's smallest mammals and require almost constant nourishment.

The larger moles, related to shrews, spend the majority of their time pursuing insects, worms, and other invertebrates below the forest leaf litter and under ground. The raised earthen tunnels of the hairy-tailed mole are often seen crossing woodland paths.

A fairly large, blackish mass situated on a tree branch may turn out to be a porcupine—a slow-moving herbivore fond of buds, new growth, and, in winter, small twigs and inner bark. The porcupine's formidable defense is well-known, but throwing quills is not in its repertoire.

The largest member of the weasel family in this region is the aquatic river otter. Otters prey chiefly on fish. Scats containing fish scales found along lake shores are often the best evidence of its presence.

A smaller relative is the mink. Its luxuriant brown fur adapts this species well for a semiaquatic existence. The mink and all weasels are efficient predators. Smaller weasels are the long- and short-tailed weasel, the latter being the smallest member of the carnivores. Consider yourself lucky if you happen upon one of these frenetic creatures along an old stone wall.

The most notorious member of the weasel family is the striped skunk, an animal that boldly advertises its malodorous defense with black-and-white coloration. Skunks, like raccoons, are omnivorous and opportunistic in their feeding habits.

Another omnivore is the black bear, the largest native mammal in this area. The regeneration of the forest has enabled the black bear population to increase markedly, and encounters between humans and bears, even in populated areas, are more common. Catching a glimpse of a bear is always a momentous event that engenders a certain amount of awe. Black bears generally are not a threat to people. They usually flee at the sight or smell of humans. Bear cubs should be given a wide berth, however. Keeping camp food away from bears will eliminate negative encounters with these magnificent animals.

The area's only feline is the bobcat, so called because of its short tail. Its great stealth makes it difficult to observe.

A recent arrival in New England is the coyote, the largest native member of the dog family. Coyotes are wary and seldom seen. Their doleful howling can sometimes be heard at night. You are much more apt to find their fur- and bone-filled scats.

As dusk falls, bats make their evening appearance, flying from roost sites in hollow trees and buildings to search for flying-insect prey. Of eight species in New England, all prodigious insect-eaters, the big brown bat and the little brown bat are the most common. Watch for bats over ponds and fields near forest, where their acrobatic maneuvers, guided by sonar, can make a fascinating show. Big brown is larger and tends to fly in a rather straight line, whereas the little brown's flight paths tend to be more erratic.

White-tailed deer are not deep-woodland inhabitants but frequent overgrown fields, "second growth" woodlands, and suburban areas. Whitetails are a rich, reddish brown in summer, but, in winter, their color changes to a grayish brown, enabling them to blend in more readily with the landscape. Most active at dawn and dusk, these browsing animals are common, but their tracks and fecal pellets are seen far more frequently than they are. The long, white underside of the tail is held straight up in flight, a signal that serves as a warning to other deer.

Few animals have a greater impact on their environment than the beaver, this region's largest rodent. The brook-damming habits of beavers are well-known. Their lodges (constructed of sticks and mud) dam water, forming ponds where these semiaquatic vegetarians safeguard themselves from predators. The ponds and the wetland plant communities created as a result of beaver activity provide habitat for many other species of wildlife. Observation at dawn and dusk is especially rewarding, as that is when beavers are most active. Beavers do not eat wood per se, but rather feed upon the nutritious inner bark of trees, stored under the ice during winter. During the warmer months, green succulent vegetation, such as yellow pond lilies, makes up their diet. Beavers live in family units that consist of parents, yearlings, and the young of the year. When beavers are two years old, they strike out on their own in search of new territory to colonize.

References

At Timberline: A Nature Guide to the Mountains of the Northeast, by F.L. Steele. Appalachian Mountain Club, Boston, 1982.

Southern New England, A Sierra Club Naturalist's Guide, by N. Jorgensen. Sierra Club Books, San Francisco, 1978.

The Stokes Nature Guide Series, Little, Brown and Company, includes guides to reptiles, amphibians, and bird behavior (three volumes), mammals.

The Petersen Field Guide Series, Houghton Mifflin Company, gives information on a wide variety of fauna, including birds, mammals, amphibians, and reptiles, animal tracks, insects, bird nests, and bird songs. *A Field Guide to Eastern Forests,* by J.C. Kricher and G. Morrison, a fairly new (1988) title in the series, uses an ecological approach.

Vegetation and Habitat
By Pam Weatherbee

The A.T. traverses a wide variety of habitats as it crosses Massachusetts and Connecticut. From the cold northern summit of Mt. Greylock to the lush open valleys of the Housatonic River, this area offers the hiker spectacular views.

Most of the land is forested now, although, 70 years ago, much of the land was abandoned farmland or had been logged. One of the most common forest types is northern hardwood, where most of the trees are sugar maple, yellow birch (with curly golden bark) or white birch, and beech, along with white ash, black cherry, red oak, and red maple. This forest usually has a luxuriant groundcover of ferns and wildflowers, spring beauty and red trillium and many violets being common in early spring. Moosewood, or striped maple, is a common small tree, noticeable by its handsome green-and-white-striped bark. Hobblebush has large, flat white flower clusters and large round leaves. The best example of this type of forest is on the slopes of Mt. Greylock, where it has been protected for more than 100 years.

As the hiker rises along the slopes to the summit of Mt. Greylock, the trees change in aspect, getting shorter with flatter, scraggly tops. Sugar maple disappears, but the birches remain, joined by spruce and fir, which are better adapted to the shorter seasons, cold, ice, and snow. The crest of Saddleball and the summit of Greylock are in the Canadian Zone, where the Montane boreal forest consists mainly of spruce and balsam fir. The Trail winds through boggy areas blanketed with sphagnum moss, edged with mountain holly and shadbush, and green with shining clubmoss and mountain woodfern. The summit trees are severely stressed in the winter by high winds blasting their bark with snow crystals. Notice the firs have luxuriant branches at the base, where they are protected by snow, while the tops are quite thin. In early summer, the mountain ashes bloom, with large showy heads of white flowers.

A change from this cold habitat is seen in the scrub oak/pitch pine forest on the open, dry ridgetops along Race Mountain and Mt. Everett. Here, the vegetation is similar to that along the New England coast. The pitch pines, especially on Mt. Everett and Pine Cobble in the northern section, are dwarfed, probably not from the severity of the weather but from very poor, acidic soil. On these and other dry ridges, such as East Mountain in Great Barrington, pitch pines, blueberry and huckleberry bushes, and occasionally bearberry, a low mat-forming shrub with shining small leaves, characterize the scene. These open ridges afford great views of the valleys, south into Connecticut and north to Mt. Greylock and Vermont.

Much of the forest on the slopes in Connecticut and south-facing slopes farther north are covered by oak-hickory forest, with red, white, black, and chestnut oaks, white pine, and shag-bark hickory common. In spring, flowering dogwood, mountain azalea, and pink lady's-slipper and, later, abundant flowers of mountain laurel fill this dry, open forest.

Sassafras, with mitten-shaped, aromatic leaves, is also found here.

The hiker will descend, especially in the hilly terrain in Connecticut, into steep-sided ravines, filled with huge boulders, where rushing streams provide a cool, moist atmosphere for the dominant hemlocks, yellow birches, occasional tulip trees (in Connecticut), and maples.

Some of the Trail passes over the Berkshire Plateau, a high, rolling plateau on the eastern side of Berkshire County with a cooler, more moist climate. Here, the forest is mixed hardwoods and hemlock, with occasional spruce and fir, particularly in the many low, swampy areas. Beaver meadows and ponds, with grasses, sedges, and dead snags, are common. Much of this forest was cut several times and is recovering. Larger ponds and lakes are more common. Goose Pond and Gore Pond are typical upland lakes, with boggy edges. Bogs, while not on the Trail, are found in this cool, swampy habitat.

Coming from the mountains into the valley brings the hiker into habitats more altered by humans. The broad valleys, smoothed by glacial action, have been cultivated and inhabited by humans for thousands of years, beginning with the native Americans, who probably arrived soon after the glaciers retreated. The two major rivers, the Hoosic and the Housatonic, have created floodplains from glacial debris and erosion. A remarkable view from the Cobbles in Cheshire, Connecticut, just before the Trail descends to the town, includes Cheshire Lake, the headwaters of the Hoosic River, and the marshes and farm fields in the valley, with the Greylock Range in the distance. In Sheffield, Massachusetts, the Housatonic has created wide floodplains of alluvial soil that are farmed extensively.

The Housatonic Valley narrows as the river enters into Connecticut, and the Trail passes through an unspoiled riverbank, river meadow, and floodplain habitat. The lush vegetation thrives on the rich, moist soil. Sycamore (with brown and white mottled bark), black willow, basswood, cottonwood, and silver maple are the common trees, along with some hickories and oaks. Riverbank grape festoons the shrubs and trees. Ostrich ferns, tall with vase-shaped clusters, form large patches. The open meadows are inhabited by grasses, sedges, iris, and huge angelica, which has coarse, ribbed stems and round, radiating flower heads.

The diversity of these habitats should enhance hikes through these areas.

Geology of Connecticut and Massachusetts
By V. Collins Chew
Excerpted from *Underfoot: A Geologic Guide to the Appalachian Trail*

With no continuous mountain chain to follow, the A.T. parallels, crosses, and recrosses rivers in Connecticut and Massachusetts and climbs the low but rugged mountains that lie along the valleys. It crosses four types of rocks with different origins, creating varying types of terrain.

In Connecticut and most of Massachusetts, the A.T. is near the south-flowing Housatonic River. Near Gore Pond, north of Dalton, Massachusetts, it crosses from the headwater area of the Housatonic to the headwaters of the north-flowing Hoosic River. The Hoosic River, which lies close to the Trail all the way to the Vermont state line, flows northwest through the southwest corner of Vermont and into upstate New York, where it joins the Hudson River. For 150 miles, the A.T. is within six miles of the Housatonic or Hoosic rivers. Nevertheless, the terrain is rugged, rocky, and scenic.

The oldest rock under the A.T. in Connecticut and Massachusetts is a billion-year-old, coarse-grained, crystalline rock composed mostly of silicate materials. Where the rock has bands of light and dark materials and breaks up into irregularly shaped blocks, it is called gneiss. Where the rock contains a great deal of mica and breaks into irregular sheets, it is called schist.

This billion-year-old rock formed during the mountain-building events and remained along the eastern edge of North America when the Iapetos Ocean opened up, in a position similar to that of the present-day Atlantic, as continents pulled apart. Between 460 and 300 million years ago, portions of this rock were caught up in other mountain-building events as the Iapetos Ocean gradually disappeared. They were thrust westward, up and over marble, to their present position on top of the marble layer. What we see is the eroded remnant of the great mass of rock that moved here. Near Pittsfield, Massachusetts, this width of crustal rock is estimated to have been reduced by 36 miles as sheet after sheet of rock was shoved over others. In Massachusetts and Connecticut, the largest remnant of this rock is called the Berkshire Highlands; a smaller section in Connecticut is called the Housatonic Highlands; at the northern edge of Massachusetts, the mountains are also formed of this rock. To the south, the Hudson Highlands and much of the Blue Ridge are also the same rock.

A second rock in the area, about half as old as the gneiss, is quartzite, once a sand beach along the coast of a sea spreading across the area. The spreading sea left a nearly continuous bed of sand, and it turned to very hard, white, pink, or yellow quartzite, which is, in many places, solid silica. Those beds are thin, but very erosion-resistant and, therefore, form high ledges above marble valleys. Earth movements carried the quartzite and other rock west over the marble. The quartzite breaks into blocky boulders, as it does at Blackrock in the Shenandoah National Park in Virginia.

Marble is a third type of rock underlying the A.T. in Connecticut and Massachusetts. Between 550 and 430 million years ago, these rocks were a lime deposit growing in a warm, clear, shallow sea on top of the sand that formed the quartzite. Mud washed in from the center of North America and formed beds of clay between the lime deposits. The area was then the continental shelf of North America, somewhat like the shelf around the Bahamas today. Subsequent mountain-building events heated and altered the lime to marble and the clay to schist, containing shiny micas, red garnets, and other crystalline materials, and contorted the beds. Erosion cut down to the marble and formed valleys that left intricate patterns of marble at the surface. The marble bedrock of these valleys is rarely seen, because it is covered with soil, clay, grit, and boulders of more resistant rock that slid down from nearby hills, dropped from melting glaciers, or was washed in by streams.

The last distinctive rock of the area is a mixture of rock types and ages, deposited as sediments in a sea to the east and later caught up in earth movements starting about 450 million years ago. The rock was shoved up and over the marble beds and other rock, or it slid down over a sloping sea floor and actually moved across the ancient rock of the Berkshire Highlands before they were uplifted. This mixture is the main rock of the Taconic Mountains, which lie mostly in New York, but the A.T. crosses the eastern outliers, Mt. Greylock and Mt. Everett in Massachusetts and Bear Mountain in Connecticut.

Heat and pressure from the earth movements hardened the sediments into schist with fairly coarse-grained minerals. Quartz veins formed in most of the rocks, and they contain enough mica to break into irregular sheets. Mt. Everett's and Bear Mountain's rocks are dark gray with white-quartz veins.

Erosion and uplift followed for many years after the mountain-building events. Several continental ice sheets later covered the area. The Hudson River Valley filled with ice first, and then tongues of ice probably flowed over low places, such as Ten Mile Valley and Macedonia Brook Valley. Then, ice from the north flowed over the whole area, covering mountain and valley alike. The ice modified the land, scraping off tens of feet of soil and some rock and gouging low basins, which later became ponds. The glaciers formed and melted many times, melting for the last time about 13,000 years ago. As they melted, they left a jumbled mass of boulders, cobbles, gravel, sand, and grit called till. This unconsolidated till is found at many places in the area.

The glaciers gouged out the Housatonic River Valley floor unevenly, leaving a chain of lakes from Falls River, Connecticut, to Pittsfield, Massachusetts. These lakes later filled with the sediments that line the entire river valley.

Massachusetts

Although it includes some strenuous climbs, most notably in the Taconics and up the state's highest mountain, Mt. Greylock, the terrain in general in Massachusetts is moderate—well-suited to day-hikes and short expeditions by novice backpackers.

Moreover, especially in southwestern Massachusetts, a wide range of available cultural activities—at the "summer homes" of many leading urban dance and theater companies—and historical sites, from battlefields to the Normal Rockwell Museum make these states ideal for those who like to break up their vacation days: a hike in the morning and concert in the evening, for example. Good sources of information on the Internet include Discover the Berkshires (<www.berkshires.org>) and the Southern Berkshire Chamber of Commerce (<www.southernberkshirechamber.com>).

Relatively shorter section-hikes are made particularly convenient by

the county's excellent public transportation system, a bus line that links the towns and cities of Adams, Cheshire, Clarksburg, Dalton, Great Barrington, Hinsdale, Lanesborough, Lee, Lenox, North Adams, Otis, Pittsfield, Richmond, Stockbridge, Washington, and Williamstown.

The Appalachian Trail runs through several of those, making possible a variety of linear hikes, with buses taken to and from the Trailheads. (For more information, contact the Berkshire Regional Transit Authority: Call (800) 292-BRTA or visit <www.berkshireta.com>.)

Western Massachusetts is an area rich in history, and it is easy to miss that as you follow the Trail. But, telltale signs are there for those who are paying attention—old cellar holes and stone walls of abandoned farms, the remnants of a settlement of Shakers, old mill ponds, mines, ruins from Massachusetts' nineteenth-century industrial boom, and, of course, monuments to battles and revolts from the early years of the United States. The Trail passes through several towns along the way, all dating back to the 1700s or earlier, and each with a rich history to be discovered in local libraries.

View of the Berkshires

Vermont to Mass. 2 (North Adams)

4.1 MILES

The northern end of this section is at the Massachusetts–Vermont line, which is also the southern terminus of Vermont's Long Trail. From there, the Trail descends, gradually and then steeply, into the valley of the Hoosic River to the towns of Williamstown and North Adams. Descending on the Trail from the southern end of the Green Mountain Range, the view is of Mt. Greylock, the Hoosac Range (Berkshire Highlands), the Taconic Range, Williamstown, and the Hoosac Valley.

Road approaches—The northern end of the section is not accessible except by the Trail. The closest road crossing is County Road in Vermont, 3.1 miles north, which is 4.5 miles from the center of Stamford, Vermont, on a marginal dirt road. The southern end is in North Adams, Massachusetts, at the intersection of Phelps Avenue and Main Street (Mass. 2). No parking is available at the Traihead but may be available 100 yards east on Mass. 2 at the Greylock Community Club; inquire first at (413) 664-9020.

Maps—Refer to ATC's Map 1 for Massachusetts–Connecticut. For area detail, consult the USGS quadrangles listed at the top right of that map.

Shelters and campsites—No shelters are located in this section, although Seth Warner Shelter in Vermont is 2.8 miles north of the section's end on a side trail. This section has one designated campsite, at Sherman Brook, mile 2.3/1.8 (0.1 mile on side trail).

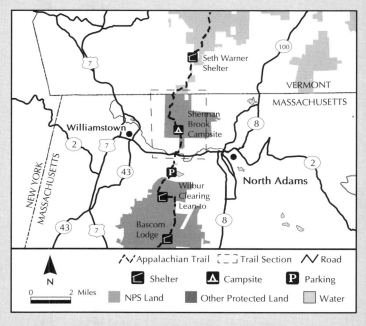

In these states, "shelter" and "lean-to" are synonymous.

Northern end of section →

There is no immediate road access to the northern end of the section, which begins high on a ridge of the Green Mountains. The nearest Trailhead northbound is in Vermont, 3.1 miles north, at County Road between Pownal and Stamford. County Road may be reached from Mill Road, which begins in Stamford. The Trailhead is 4.5 miles from the center of Stamford on a rough dirt road. (See *Appalachian Trail Guide to New Hampshire–Vermont*.)

Long Trail →

The Long Trail (maintained by the Green Mountain Club) coincides with the Appalachian Trail for 103 miles in Vermont and then continues north to the Canadian border. It was the first true U.S. long-distance hiking trail, with construction beginning in 1910, and was an inspiration for Benton MacKaye's proposal of the Appalachian Trail in 1921.

Clarksburg State Forest →

A 2,933-acre tract of undisturbed land, popular with hunters, near Clarksburg State Park. There is no connecting trail from the A.T. to the park's camping and hiking areas.

Eph's Lookout →

"Eph" was Col. Ephraim Williams, Jr., killed in a 1755 ambush during the French and Indian War. Williams had owned property along the Hoosic, west of Fort Massachusetts (now the site of a Price Chopper supermarket, less than half a mile from the A.T.), and had been in charge of the region's defense during the fighting. In his will, he provided for the founding of what was probably meant to be a free village school, but which became Williams College in the years after the Revolutionary War. The town there, known as West Township or West Hoosuck, was named Williamstown after him in 1765.

N-S

TRAIL DESCRIPTION

0.0 The Massachusetts line, the **northern end of section,** is 3.1 miles south of the nearest Trailhead, on County Road in Vermont. A register, a **Long Trail** historic sign, and a "Welcome to Massachusetts" sign are all on the Vermont–Massachusetts border. ■ NORTHBOUND hikers follow the A.T. and Long Trail (L.T.), which follow a single route northward for more than 100 miles along the Green Mountains (see *Appalachian Trail Guide to New Hampshire–Vermont*). — **4.1**

0.3 Bear Swamp and brook, in **Clarksburg State Forest**, is 0.25 mile off the Trail to the east; it is one of the sources of Hudson Brook, which goes through Natural Bridge State Park in North Adams. — **3.8**

0.5 Abandoned road descends west to Henderson Road in Williamstown. — **3.6**

0.8 Pass by **Eph's Lookout**, a quartzite ridge with a limited view west to Williamstown and the Taconic mountain range along the New York border. — **3.3**

North Adams

S-N

SECTION HIGHLIGHTS

Class of '98 Trail →

Blazed blue, this trail leads approximately 2 miles down the west side of East Mountain and connects to the Pine Cobble Trail approximately 0.75 mile from North Hoosic Road, thus forming a loop trail that takes in views from Pine Cobbles as well as some of the upland areas traversed by the A.T. (See page 171.)

Pine Cobble Trail →

Blazed blue, this trail leads 2.1 miles down the south side of East Mountain to the rock outcropping known as Pine Cobble and then descends farther into Williamstown at Williams College's Pine Cobble Development, near North Hoosac Road. Extensive blueberry bushes are found at the junction of this trail and the A.T. (See page 170.)

Bog →

Upcountry bogs of sphagnum (or peat) moss are common in New England, but less so south of the Green Mountains, and are fragile ecological systems. The dead cells of the sphagnum plants can hold up to 20 times their weight in water.

Bad-weather trail →

In wet or icy weather, this 0.3-mile trail allows hikers to bypass a steep boulder field of pink quartzite.

Sherman Brook Campsite →

Accessible *via* a 0.1-mile side trail, the campsite includes three tent platforms and a privy. Campfires permitted in designated locations. Water available at nearby Pete's Spring or Sherman Brook.

N-S

| | TRAIL DESCRIPTION | |

1.0	Pass the blue-blazed **Class of '98 Trail**, built in 1998 by the Williams College Outing Club, leading to the west to make a loop with the **Pine Cobble Trail**. The woods here are abundant in the spring with wildflowers, including lady's-slippers, pink azalea, and sheep's laurel.	**3.1**
1.3	At East Mountain, the blue-blazed **Pine Cobble Trail** coming in from the south intersects with the A.T. A quartzite-covered viewpoint is 200 feet south on the Pine Cobble Trail.	**2.8**
1.4	Trail skirts north side of a sphagnum-moss **bog**.	**2.7**
1.5	At a good view of the Hoosac Range, east of Mt. Greylock, the northern end of a blue-blazed **bad-weather trail** intersects on the west side of A.T., which descends steeply over a quartzite boulder field.	**2.6**
1.7	Southern end of a blue-blazed bad-weather trail intersects on the west side of A.T.	**2.4**
2.3	Blue-blazed side trail to **Sherman Brook Campsite** intersects the west side of the A.T. in the midst of patches of mountain laurel.	**1.8**
2.5	Blue-blazed side trail to Sherman Brook Campsite intersects on west side of Trail. Pete's Spring is on east side of A.T. across from the intersection.	**1.6**

Textile mills →

The cities of North Adams and Pittsfield were among Massachusetts' most prominent industrial areas in the late nineteenth century. Massachusetts was one of the first states to industrialize, and, at the time of the outbreak of the Civil War, it was the second-most densely populated state in the nation—much of that due to its booming textile and shoe plants. When these jobs went south in the early twentieth century, the economic impact to North Adams was severe.

Boston & Maine Railroad →

East of North Adams, the former B&M passes through the four-mile-long Hoosac Tunnel, beneath the Hoosac Range. Completed in 1875 through one of the earliest industrial uses of a new explosive, nitroglycerin, it was for many years the longest rail tunnel in the United States. Now operated by a transportation conglomerate, the B&M carried passengers until 1970 and at one time ran the Boston subway system. The Trail crosses the railway on a footbridge just north of the Hoosic River.

Southern end of section →

At Mass. 2, the highway between the towns of Williamstown (west) and North Adams (east). North Adams is a large town with museums, stores, restaurants, and many services, including bus service. Several major stores are within a short walk of the Trail in either direction along Mass. 2. There is no parking at the Trailhead, but overnight parking may be available 100 yards east of the A.T. on Mass. 2 at the Greylock Community Club; inquire first at (413) 664-9020.

N-S

	TRAIL DESCRIPTION	

2.9 A.T. crosses Clarksburg State Forest boundary close to Sherman Brook.   **1.2**

3.0 The Trail goes through 0.4 mile of hemlock groves alongside Sherman Brook.   **1.1**

3.5 Trail passes under high-voltage powerline. Blackberries can found there in summer.   **0.6**

3.7 Trail crosses Sherman Brook twice, passing an old dam, spillway, pipe, and rails that were part of the complex of **textile mills** in the Hoosic River valley, long abandoned.   **0.4**

3.8 Trail intersects with Massachusetts Avenue in North Adams. ■ Southbound hikers follow the road west toward Hoosic River footbridge. ■ Northbound hikers follow a driveway near a house uphill toward the woods.   **0.3**

3.9 Footbridge across the **Boston & Maine Railroad** and the Hoosic River (lowest point of A.T. in Massachusetts at 640 feet). ■ Northbound hikers cross footbridge to Massachusetts Avenue and follow road east. ■ Southbound hikers cross river on footbridge.   **0.2**

4.1 The **southern end of section** is in North Adams at the intersection of Phelps Avenue and Mass. 2 (Main Street). ■ Northbound hikers continue toward footbridge across the Hoosic River. ■ Southbound hikers follow Phelps Avenue uphill toward Mt. Williams (see Massachusetts Section 2).   **0.0**

S-N

Mass. 2 (North Adams) to Cheshire

14.0 MILES

The Trail leads from North Adams and the Hoosac Valley up the north slopes of Mt. Greylock (3,491 feet), the highest mountain in Massachusetts and the highest point on the Trail between Vermont and Virginia. At the heart of this section is the 13,500-acre Mt. Greylock State Reservation, the state's first, which has a 70-mile trail system. The Trail descends from Mt. Greylock and passes through the town of Cheshire at the southern end of the section.

Road approaches—The northern end of this section is in North Adamas at the intersection of Phelps Avenue and Mass. 2 (Main Street), without parking. Overnight parking may be available at Greylock Community Center on Mass. 2, 100 yards to the east; inquire first at (413) 664-9020. The southern end is on Mass. 8 in the town of Cheshire; no parking is available there but can be found 0.6 mile south on the Trail at Church Street. Vehicular access is also available at Pattison Road (mile 0.9/13.1; small parking lot on northern side); Notch Road (mile 3.1/10.9, with day-use parking 100 yards south); the junction of Notch, Rockwell, and Summit roads a half-mile south of the Mt. Greylock summit (mile 6.8/7.2, with gravel parking lot to east); and lower on Rockwell Road (miles 7.0/7.0 and 7.3/6.7, with parking lot near the latter). For day-use parking and accommodations at Mt. Greylock, see page 62.

Maps—Refer to ATC's Map 1 for Massachusetts–Connecticut. For area detail, consult the USGS quadrangles listed at the top right of that map.

Shelters and Campsites—Wilbur Clearing Shelter is at mile 3.0/11.0, down a side trail. The Mark Noepel Shelter, located on a side trail near Bassett Brook, is at mile 9.6/4.4. Camping is prohibited in the North Adams–Mt. Williams Reservoir watershed on the northern side of the Mt. Greylock massif. Three non-A.T. shelters are within a mile of the Trail in the Mt. Greylock Reservation.

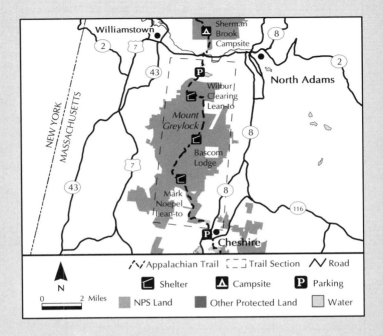

Williamstown

North Adams

Sherman Brook Campsite

Wilbur Clearing Lean-to

Mount Greylock

Bascom Lodge

Mark Noepel Lean-to

Cheshire

NEW YORK
MASSACHUSETTS

N

0   2 Miles

/\/ Appalachian Trail   [_] Trail Section   /\/ Road

Shelter   Campsite   P Parking

NPS Land   Other Protected Land   Water

SECTION HIGHLIGHTS

Northern end of section →

On Mass. 2, the highway between the towns of Williamstown (west) and North Adams (east). North Adams is a large town with stores, restaurants, and many services, including bus transportation. Several major stores are within a short walk of the Trail in either direction along Mass. 2. There is no parking at the Trailhead, but overnight parking may be available 100 yards east of the A.T. on Mass. 2 at the Greylock Community Club; inquire first at (413) 664-9020. Parking also is available on Pattison Road, 0.9 mile south from the beginning of the section.

Pattison Road →

Leads past Mt. Williams Reservoir and a huge water treatment plant. A small A.T. parking lot is on the northern side; a Norway spruce plantation, on the southern side.

Mt. Prospect Trail →

Leads south 0.6 mile to summit of Mt. Prospect and down the mountain's southern side, where it meets up with the Money Brook Trail. At the A.T. intersection, hikers can enjoy a precipitous view of farms to the west along Williamstown's Green River Valley and of the New York–Massachusetts border, including Berlin Mountain (2,798 feet), the highest of the Taconic range.

N-S

TRAIL DESCRIPTION

0.0 The **northern end of section** is at the junction of Phelps   **14.0**
Avenue with Mass. 2 in North Adams. Facing south from
here, there are good views of Mt. Williams on the left and
Mt. Prospect on the right. Paull Brook leads down from
the slopes in between, a historic valley that was the site
of early iron mining. ■ NORTHBOUND hikers cross the railroad and the Hoosic River on a footbridge (see Massachusetts Section 1). ■ SOUTHBOUND hikers proceed up
Phelps Avenue.

0.4 At Phelps Avenue and Catherine Street, the Vermont-   **13.6**
border hills of Pine Cobble and Eph's Lookout, at the
southern extent of the Green Mountains, can be seen to
the north.

0.5 A.T. intersects with steep driveway called Phelps Avenue   **13.5**
Extension. ■ SOUTHBOUND hikers turn sharply left and enter
woods from the paved drive. ■ NORTHBOUND hikers follow
pavement to Phelps Avenue.

0.7 A local off-road-vehicle trail crosses the A.T.   **13.3**

0.9 Trail crosses **Pattison Road**.   **13.1**

1.7 Trail crosses the boundary between Mt. Greylock State   **12.3**
Reservation and the North Adams watershed on the steep,
hemlock-covered, north-facing ridge of Mt. Prospect. No
camping north of here.

2.8 ■ SOUTHBOUND hikers turn sharply left. **Mt. Prospect Trail**   **11.2**
intersects on west side of A.T. When the wind is from the
west, hang-gliders sometimes use a summit ledge as a
launching place. From the ledge, expansive views are
available to the west of the Taconics and Williamstown.

S-N

Wilbur Clearing Shelter →

Reached *via* Money Brook Trail, 0.3 mile south of A.T. Accommodates six. An intermittent spring is nearby, as are a privy, a fire pit, tent platforms, and earthen tent pads. Next shelter: south, 7.1 miles (Mark Noepel); north, 10.4 miles (Seth Warner). Money Brook Trail continues 3.75 miles south and west to Hopper Road (see page 176).

Notch Road →

Swings around the summit of Mt. Greylock on the northern and western sides of the mountain. Also accessible where the A.T. descends from the Greylock summit 3.5 miles farther south by Trail from this crossing. The northern Trail crossing of Notch Road is located in the level saddle between Mt. Prospect and Mt. Williams where Wilbur Farm stood in the 1800s. A day-use-only parking lot is 100 yards south of the intersection, and a reliable spring is 0.25 mile north, downhill along the road. Parking (day-use only) is also available near the southern crossing of Notch Road (see mile 6.8/7.2).

Mt. Williams →

The view to the northeast from Mt. Williams is of the nearby Hoosic Range, the Green Mountains, and the Vermont ski areas of Mt. Snow and Mt. Haystack.

Bernard Farm Trail →

Leads 3.0 miles east toward the park gate on Notch Road in North Adams. A 0.3-mile short-cut leads west to Notch Road.

N-S

TRAIL DESCRIPTION

3.0 Money Brook Trail intersects on west side of A.T. in a **11.0**
red-spruce grove. **Wilbur Clearing Shelter** is 0.3 mile
south from here on the Money Brook Trail.

3.1 Trail intersects with **Notch Road**. **10.9**

3.2 At the eastern edge of a red-spruce grove, farmer Jeremi- **10.8**
ah Wilbur's original road toward the summit can be
discerned crossing the A.T.

4.0 Summit of **Mt. Williams** (2,951 feet), with register box. **10.0**

4.2 At a four-way junction, the blue-blazed **Bernard Farm** **9.8**
Trail intersects with A.T. on the east side in saddle between Mt. Williams and Mt. Fitch (3,110 feet).

5.0 Trail crosses unusual outcropping of milky quartz atop **9.0**
Mt. Fitch.

Eastern painted turtle

S-N

Thunderbolt, Bellows Pipe, and Robinson Point trails →

The Thunderbolt and Bellows Pipe trails both go steeply down the eastern side of the mountain. Thunderbolt, which leads toward Adams, was originally a popular downhill ski trail, now used only for hiking, telemark skiing, and snowboarding. An overnight shelter for backpackers, Bellows Pipe Lean-to, is one mile down the Bellows Pipe Trail, which leads to Notch Road in North Adams. A short, 0.1-mile connector trail goes west, crossing Notch Road to the Robinson Point Trail, which leads to a westward-facing overlook of the ravine known as the Hopper. (See page 171.)

Mt. Greylock →

Originally, the Mt. Greylock massif was known locally as "Saddle-back Mountain," with "Greylock" originating in the 1840s. Saddle Ball Mountain marked its southern end. The A.T. crosses Summit Road on the northern side of the peak, separated from the parking lot and a wheelchair-accessible pavilion by 200 feet of trail. The summit is 16 miles from Pittsfield by Rockwell Road and nine miles from North Adams by Notch Road. See also page 64. *Alcohol possession or consumption is illegal within the Mt. Greylock reservation.*

War Memorial Tower →

This 93-foot-high structure, built in 1932, originally was intended to be a lighthouse along the Charles River in Boston. Visitors can ascend an internal staircase for a 360-degree view of the northern Berkshires, New York, and Vermont. On extremely clear days, sunlight reflecting off the towers in Boston is said to be visible on the eastern horizon.

Bascom Lodge →

Built in 1937 as a Civilian Conservation Corps project, the lodge remains a popular mountaintop accommodation and is listed on the National Register of Historic Places. Reservations are recommended (see page 64). Stone walls, landscaping, paved pathways, and coin-operated viewers surround the War Memorial Tower and the lodge.

N-S

TRAIL DESCRIPTION

5.8 A.T. intersects with **Thunderbolt Trail** and **Bellows Pipe Trail** to the east, and a short connecting trail to the **Robinson Point Trail** and Notch Road to the west, all within 100 yards of each other. **8.2**

6.3 Summit of **Mt. Greylock** (3,491 feet), highest point in Massachusetts with climatic conditions similar to northern Canada. The **War Memorial Tower** and **Bascom Lodge** are at the summit. On the southwest side, the A.T. goes past an antenna for a television-and-radio station and some composting privies. **7.7**

War Memorial Tower

S-N

Gould Trail →

Leads east from a day-use parking area at the junction of Notch, Rockwell, and Summit roads down toward the town of Adams. An overnight backpacker's shelter, Pecks Brook Lean-to, is one mile from the trailhead. (See page 174.)

Cheshire Harbor Trail, Hopper Trail →

The Cheshire Harbor Trail (mountain bike/snowmobiling) leads 1.6 miles to the Old Adams Road trail, east of Mt. Greylock. The Hopper Trail leads to the Sperry Road Campground (with overnight parking), just over a mile to the west. (See pages 172 and 174.)

Rockwell Road →

An important vehicular route to Summit Road and the top of the mountain. Leads south toward Lanesborough and the Mt. Greylock Visitors Center.

Jones Nose Trail →

Leads south in 1.0 mile to a parking lot on Rockwell Road.

Mark Noepel Shelter →

Named after a former thru-hiker, ridgerunner, and naturalist. Reached by way of a 0.2-mile side trail leading down to the shelter. Shelter accommodates 16. Two tent platforms, fire pit, privy, and an intermittent spring are nearby. Next shelter: south, 17.1 miles (Kay Wood); north, 7.1 miles (Wilbur Clearing).

Old Adams Road →

The A.T. crosses mountain-bike, horse, and snowmobile trails at Old Adams Road, which leads west two miles to Jones Nose Trail at Rockwell Road. Just east of the intersection is the spot where Old Adams Road intersects with the historic Red Gate Road Trail to Cheshire. Neither is open to automobiles.

N-S	TRAIL DESCRIPTION	

6.8	Trail crosses junction of Notch, Rockwell, and Summit roads. An old water-supply pond and pumphouse are on the A.T. south of this junction. East of this junction is a gravel parking lot and the trailhead for the **Gould Trail**.	7.2
6.9	Intersection with blue-blazed **Hopper Trail**, which descends west to Sperry Campground.	7.1
7.0	Intersection with Rockwell Road and the **Cheshire Harbor Trail**, which descends to the east.	7.0
7.3	Meet **Rockwell Road** (for the first or last time) at top of hairpin curve; gravel parking lot and free-swinging A.T. sign are nearby.	6.7
7.4	View of Greylock is just north of bog bridges over a sphagnum-moss bog popular with bird-watchers.	6.6
7.5	Northern end of ridge of Saddle Ball Mountain. *For southbound hikers, intermittent, swamp-fed streams here are only water source for the next several miles.*	6.5
9.0	Blue-blazed **Jones Nose Trail** intersects with A.T. on southern end of Saddle Ball Mountain summit.	5.0
9.6	Blue-blazed side trail to **Mark Noepel Shelter**, near the headwaters of a tributary of Bassett Brook.	4.4
10.5	Cross **Old Adams Road**.	3.5
11.5	Pass view to the southeast from an open ledge above Kitchen Brook drainage.	2.5

S-N

SECTION HIGHLIGHTS

Kitchen Brook →

Named for its use in the mid-1800s as a feeding-place for escaped slaves on the Underground Railroad. A viewpoint overlooking the drainage is a few steps west of the trail.

Southern end of section →

At Mass. 8, which runs from Cheshire to Adams. No parking available at Trailhead. A convenience store is 0.2 mile south on Mass. 8. Groceries, lodging, restaurants, a post office, and other services are available in Cheshire (ZIP Code 01225); an outfitter is located along the road in Adams, several miles north of the A.T. Bus service is available. Parking is available at the Ashuwillticook Rail-Trail crossing at Railroad Street in Cheshire (see Massachusetts Section Three).

Accommodations on Mt. Greylock

Bascom Lodge, a rustic stone-and-wood facility located on the Trail at the summit of Mt. Greylock 6.3 miles from the northern end of the section, offers overnight accommodations, along with telephones, toilets, and a restaurant; (413) 743-1591. Some of the finest views of the Berkshires can be had through the wrap-around windows of the enclosed porch. Reservations are required for breakfast and dinner at the privately managed lodge, renovated and upgraded in 2007–9 and now home to two new eateries.

Mt. Greylock State Reservation is open all year from sunrise until dark for day-use recreation, and overnight camping and lodging is allowed May–December at designated sites and the lodge. Roads to

N-S

TRAIL DESCRIPTION

12.4   A.T. follows a hemlock ridge with a steep drop-off to   **1.6**
Kitchen Brook Valley to the west.

13.0   Cross under powerlines.   **1.0**

13.2   Cross Outlook Avenue between hayfields. A curious   **0.8**
rock-and-tree formation called Reynolds Rock is along
the southeastern side of the road crossing.

14.0   **Southern end of section** is where the Trail intersects Mass.   **0.0**
8 in Cheshire. The open hayfields leading down to the
road here afford a nice view of the Cheshire Cobbles south
of town. ▪ SOUTHBOUND hikers cross Mass. 8 and follow
Trail through open field between Mass. 8 on the north
and School Street on the south, turning right onto School
Street (see Massachusetts Section 3). ▪ NORTHBOUND hikers
climb through hayfields away from highway.

S-N

the summit of Mt. Greylock usually are open from May 15 to November 1 (December 1 to December 15, hunters only). For further information, including information about the winter road, call (413) 499-4262 or visit <www.mass.gov/dcr/parks/mtgreylock>. Overnight parking is allowed only at Sperry Road Campground (Rockwell Road) and in the Mt. Greylock summit parking lot ($2 fee).

Although all months are popular at Mt. Greylock, fall-foliage months are especially crowded, so plan ahead. Changes in lead color begin to intensify in late September, with peak color about the second week of October. Up-to-date reports are available on the Web at <www.yankeefoliage.com>. Guidance on attractions throughout this area can be found at <www.berkshires.org>, and detailed information on Mt. Greylock is available at <www.mass.gov/dcr/parks/mtGreylock>.

Cheshire to Dalton

9.3 MILES

Much of the Trail land in this section was obtained through the generosity of the Crane family of Dalton. The papers for U.S. currency and other fine papers are still produced in its mills. Between the towns of Cheshire to the north and Dalton to the south, the Trail crosses the plateau of the southern Hoosac Range (Berkshire Highlands) and the divide between two important Massachusetts watersheds. Cheshire is in the watershed of the west-flowing Hoosic River, at the foot of the scenic Cheshire Cobbles. Dalton is in the watershed of the south-flowing Housatonic River, at the foot of North Mountain.

Road approaches—The northern end of this section is on Mass. 8 in the town of Cheshire; no parking is available there but can be found 0.6 mile south on the Trail at the Ashuwillticook Rail-Trail crossing of the A.T. at Railroad Street. Access and parking also is available at mile 8.3/1.0 on Gulf Road/High Street entering Dalton; that is the parking, too, for the southern end of the section at the junction of High Street with Mass 8 & 9 in the center of Dalton.

Maps—Refer to ATC's Map 1 for Massachusetts–Connecticut. For area detail, consult the USGS quadrangles listed at the top right of that map.

Shelters and campsites—There are no shelters between Cheshire and Dalton. Open fires are allowed only at Crystal Mountain Campsite, the section's only designated camping area, halfway between the two towns.

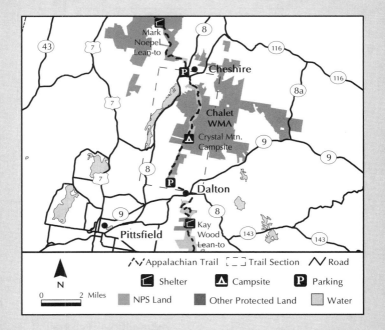

Northern end of section →

On Mass. 8, which runs from Cheshire to Adams. No parking is available at Trailhead. A convenience store is 0.2 mile south on Mass. 8. Groceries, lodging, restaurants, a post office, and other services are available in Cheshire (ZIP Code 01225); an outfitter is located along the road in Adams, several miles north of the A.T. Bus service is available. Parking is available at the Ashuwillticook rail-trail on Church Street in Cheshire (see mile 0.6/8.7).

Replica of cheese press →

On the southern side of the intersection of Church and School streets is the Cheshire post office. On the northern side is an unusual monument: a giant cheese press. During the 1802 presidential election, Cheshire (then a dairy center) was the only Berkshire County town that Thomas Jefferson carried. When Jefferson won, to pay homage to him, the town fathers decided to send a gift in the form of a Cheshire cheese—one using curds from every farmer in town. The result was a cheese wheel four feet across, eighteen inches high, and weighing 1,235 pounds. A sled drawn by six horses took it east to be shipped off to Washington, D.C., where it drew a personal letter of thanks from President Jefferson.

Ashuwillticook Rail-Trail →

Making use of an abandoned railroad bed, this 11.2-mile bike-ski-and-pedestrian trail connects the towns of Lanesborough and Adams. It is one of the most popular trails in the region.

The Cobbles →

A short side trail on top of the ridge leads to Cheshire Cobbles, a series of white-quartzite ledges, and affords a spectacular view of Mt. Greylock rising out of the Hoosic River Valley. Notice the grooves in the rock that testify to the action of glaciers.

N-S

TRAIL DESCRIPTION

0.0 **Northern end of section** is on south side of Mass. 8, 0.5 mile from the center of Cheshire. ■ SOUTHBOUND hikers follow Trail through open field between Mass. 8 on the north and School Street on the south, turning right onto School Street. ■ NORTHBOUND hikers cross Mass. 8 and climb through hayfields away from highway (see Massachusetts Section 2). **9.3**

0.5 Pass **replica of cheese press** at intersection of School Street and Church Street. ■ SOUTHBOUND hikers turn left on Church Street. ■ NORTHBOUND hikers turn right onto School Street. **8.8**

0.6 Follow Church Street across the **Ashuwillticook Rail-Trail** that goes between Lanesboro Mall in Pittsfield and the town of Adams. **8.7**

0.7 Church Street intersects with Furnace Hill Road. ■ SOUTHBOUND hikers turn right and follow Furnace Hill Road south. ■ NORTHBOUND hikers turn left and follow Church Street west. **8.6**

0.9 Trail intersects with private driveway. ■ SOUTHBOUND hikers leave driveway and climb left toward the Cobbles. ■ NORTHBOUND hikers turn right onto Furnace Hill Road, a short, steep residential connector between the center of Cheshire and the base of the Cobbles. **8.4**

1.7 Blue-blazed side trail to **the Cobbles**. **7.6**

S-N

SECTION HIGHLIGHTS

North Mountain →

The mostly level, wooded, boggy upland of North Mountain is typical of the Berkshire Highlands between Mt. Greylock and the Housatonic Valley.

Gore Pond →

A glacially formed pond, which beaver activity sometimes deepens. Its waters are darkened by tannins from the humus, and a recent U.S. Environmental Protection Agency assessment listed its water quality as poor, due in part to noxious plants. No camping is permitted at the pond.

N-S

TRAIL DESCRIPTION

1.8 Near top of the southernmost cobble, pass a bronze USGS marker set into the ledge. From here to Dalton, the Trail runs mostly along the plateau of **North Mountain**. **7.5**

2.4 Pass east of a granite marker at the boundary between Cheshire and Dalton. **6.9**

3.7 Cross old logging road left by J.W. Cowee Lumber Co., now controlled by the Massachusetts Division of Fish and Wildlife and used as a snowmobile route in the winter. **5.6**

4.2 Cross outlet of **Gore Pond**, which usually supports a family of beavers that try to flood the trail with their dams. **5.2**

Red eft near Gore Pond

S-N

Crystal Mountain Campsite →

Water supply is at an intermittent brook crossed on the A.T. A privy is available. Campfires permitted at designated campsite only.

Dalton →

This small Massachusetts town (population 7,000) was founded about the time of the Revolution and afterward became drawn into the uprising known as Shays' Rebellion, in which several Dalton residents played important roles (see Massachusetts Section 9). After the protest was put down, a local history reports, the town was more severely punished for its part in the revolt than others in the county. Today, it is notable mostly for its paper-making. Crane & Company, one of two major manufacturers here, underwrites the Crane Museum of paper-making on Main Street, open afternoons during the summer. The town is very "hiker friendly" and has many services available.

Southern end of section →

Overnight parking available at the lot on Gulf Road in Dalton, reached by following High Street northwest from intersection of Mass. 8 and 9. Dalton (ZIP Code 01226) offers most services to hikers, including laundry, grocery, lodging, post office, and restaurants. Bus service is available.

TRAIL DESCRIPTION

4.6 Blue-blazed trail leads east at an intermittent brook, the water supply for **Crystal Mountain Campsite**. **4.7**

5.0 Pass under powerline. Black bears frequently have been seen here, sampling a variety of seasonal berries. **4.3**

8.3 At foot of North Mountain, cross parking lot on Gulf Road, which becomes High Street. Parking here for southern end of section at a kiosk-style bulletin board set up amongst the hemlocks. ■ SOUTHBOUND hikers follow High Street into **Dalton**. ■ NORTHBOUND hikers leave streets and enter woods. **1.0**

8.4 Cross Park Avenue. **0.9**

9.3 **Southern end of section** at junction of High Street with Mass. 8 and 9, in the center of Dalton. Parking is a mile north on Gulf Road. ■ SOUTHBOUND hikers follow Mass. 8 east from Dalton (see Massachusetts Section 4). ■ NORTHBOUND hikers follow High Street west. **0.0**

S-N

Dalton to Pittsfield Road

9.6 MILES

Old cellar holes and the stone walls of abandoned farms can be found along this section. The abandoned fierlds grew into forests and are now part of the Pittsfield watershed. Like Section Three, much of this one is relatively flat, running along the swampy highlands of the Berkshire Plateau. Except for a few rocky and steep portions in the middle and the northern end, it is mostly level, wet, and suitable for cross-country skiing in snowy months. The views from Warner Hill are especially nice after the leaves fall.

Road approaches—The northern end of this section is at the junction of High Street with Mass 8 & 9 in the center of Dalton, with parking one mile north on the Trail at Gulf Road (which High Street becomes). The southern end is off Pittsfield Road (also called Washington Mountain Road) about eight miles east of Pittsfield and five miles northwest of Beckett. Parking is available at the Trail crossing, and access and limited parking is available at mile 6.4/3.2, Blotz Road, six miles east of Pittsfield and 1.3 miles west of Mass. 8.

Maps—Refer to ATC's Map 1 for Massachusetts–Connecticut. For area detail, consult the USGS quadrangles listed at the top right of that map.

Shelters and campsites—This section has one shelter, Kay Wood Shelter, at mile 3.0/6.6 and 0.2 mile east on a side trail.

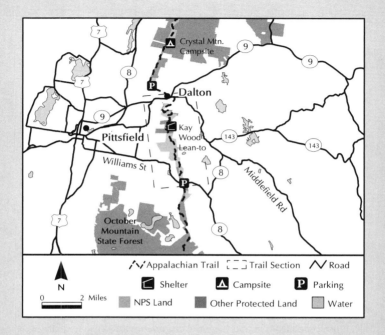

Appalachian Trail   Trail Section   Road

Shelter   Campsite   Parking

N

0   2 Miles

NPS Land   Other Protected Land   Water

Northern end of section →

Overnight parking available at the lot on Gulf Road in Dalton, reached by following High Street northwest from intersection of Mass. 8 and 9. Dalton (ZIP Code 01226) offers most services to hikers, including laundry, grocery, lodging, post office, and restaurants. Bus service is available.

Dalton →

This small Massachusetts town (population 7,000) was founded about the time of the Revolution and afterward became drawn into the uprising known as Shays' Rebellion, in which several Dalton residents played important roles (see Massachusetts Section 9). After the protest was put down, a local history reports, the town was more severely punished for its part in the revolt than others in the county. Today, it is notable mostly for its paper-making. Crane & Company, one of two major manufacturers here, underwrites the Crane Museum of paper-making on Main Street, open afternoons during the summer. The town is very "hiker friendly" and has many services available.

Housatonic River →

An important river to Massachusetts and Connecticut residents, the Housatonic has its source near the community of Hinsdale, east of Dalton. The A.T. generally parallels the river valley south into Connecticut. It was an important reason for the development of nearby Pittsfield, the largest city in the region and an industrial center for western Massachusetts. Some parts of the river have suffered serious pollution from that development.

N-S

┌─────────────────────────────┐
│ TRAIL DESCRIPTION │
└─────────────────────────────┘

0.0 **Northern end of section** at junction of High Street with Mass. 8 and 9, in the center of town. Parking for the northern end of section is a mile north of the end of the section, on Gulf Road, which is what High Street becomes. ■ SOUTHBOUND hikers follow Mass. 8 east from **Dalton**. ■ NORTHBOUND hikers follow High Street west. (See Massachusetts Section 3)   **9.6**

0.2 Junction of Depot Street and Mass. 8. ■ SOUTHBOUND hikers follow Depot Street south. ■ NORTHBOUND hikers follow Mass. 8 west across the **Housatonic River**.   **9.4**

0.5 Cross intersection of Housatonic Street and Depot Street.   **9.1**

0.6 Cross railroad tracks at foot of Day Mountain. This is an active line, so pay special attention to rails that curve out of sight to the west. ■ SOUTHBOUND hikers begin climb up Day Mountain. ■ NORTHBOUND hikers follow Depot Street into Dalton.   **9.0**

2.5 Trail follows and crosses a hemlock-laden ravine just below junction of two brooks.   **7.1**

S-N

Grange Hall Road →

Leads west into western edge of Dalton, at its border with the city of Pittsfield. Limited roadside parking is available here.

Kay Wood Shelter →

Named after a longtime Trail maintainer, one of the original members of the Massachusetts A.T. Committee, and a thru-hiker. This shelter accommodates 16. A privy is nearby. The water source is an intermittent brook on a blue-blazed trail down a steep bank in front of the shelter. Next shelter: south, 9.0 miles (October Mountain); north, 17.1 miles (Mark Noepel).

Pittsfield →

The chief city of western Massachusetts, with a population of about 80,000 in its metropolitan area, Pittsfield was founded in 1752 and incorporated in 1761. It was named for English Prime Minister William Pitt. During the eighteenth and ninteenth centuries, the water-power of the nearby Housatonic made it an important center for both farming and industry.

Blotz Road →

The paved road leads west six miles to Pittsfield and east 1.3 miles to Mass. 8. Limited parking is available here; not recommended for overnight parking.

Southern end of section →

Reached *via* paved Pittsfield Road (also called Washington Mountain Road), eight miles from Pittsfield and five miles from Becket. No public transportation or accommodations are available. Parking is available at a lot at the Trail crossing.

N-S

TRAIL DESCRIPTION

2.7 Trail crosses **Grange Hall Road**.   **6.9**

3.0 Blue-blazed side trail leads 0.2 mile east to **Kay Wood Shelter**.   **6.6**

3.1 Cross under powerlines with view of **Pittsfield**, five miles to the west.   **6.5**

5.7 Summit of Warner Hill (2,050 feet) is just off the trail to the east. Hikers may find blueberries here in the summer and a view of Mt. Greylock to the north.   **3.9**

6.4 Cross **Blotz Road** through a small parking lot on the north side. ■ SOUTHBOUND hikers enter a three-mile section of narrow Trail corridor through the city of Pittsfield's watershed that crosses many bog-bridged wet areas and small streams, with only one short, cliffy section.   **3.2**

9.6 The **southern end of section** at Pittsfield Road can be identified by a large A.T. sign mounted between posts. ■ NORTHBOUND hikers enter a three-mile section of narrow Trail corridor through the city of Pittsfield's watershed that crosses many bog-bridged wet areas and small streams, with only one short, cliffy section. ■ SOUTHBOUND hikers cross Pittsfield Road to a dirt road for the Pittsfield watershed area (see Massachusetts Section 5).   **0.0**

S-N

Pittsfield Road to U.S. 20 (Jacob's Ladder Highway)

9.4 MILES

This section has varied terrain but little change in elevation, as it runs along the plateau of the Hoosac Range (the Berkshire Highlands). It passes through parts of October Mountain State Forest, skirts Finerty Pond, and has a short, steep climb up Walling and Becket mountains.

Road approaches—The northern end of this section is off Pittsfield Road (also called Washington Mountain Road) about eight miles east of Pittsfield and five miles northwest of Beckett. Parking is available at the Trail crossing. The southern end on U.S. 20 five miles east of Lee has a parking lot 100 yards to the west. Vehicular access also may be possible on dirt West Branch Road (mile 1.5/7.9) or County Road (mile 4.0/5.4) four miles west of Mass. 8.

Maps—Refer to ATC's Map 1 for Massachusetts–Connecticut. For area detail, consult the USGS quadrangles listed at the top right of that map.

Shelters and campsites—No camping is permitted except at October Mountain Shelter, the only designated shelter/campsite in the section, at mile 2.2/7.2 on a short side trail.

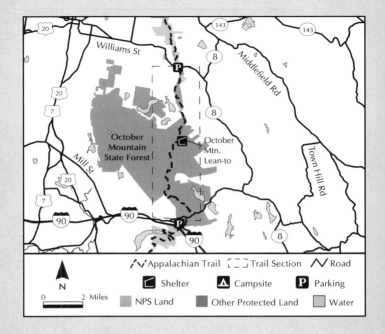

Williams St

October
Mountain
State Forest

October
Mtn.
Lean-to

Middlefield Rd

Town Hill Rd

Mill St

Appalachian Trail   Trail Section   Road

N
0   2 Miles

Shelter   Campsite   Parking

NPS Land   Other Protected Land   Water

SECTION HIGHLIGHTS

Northern end of section →

Reached *via* paved Pittsfield Road (also called Washington Mountain Road), eight miles from Pittsfield and five miles from Becket. No public transportation or accommodations are available. Parking available at a lot at the Trail crossing.

October Mountain State Forest →

At 14,189 acres, the largest state forest in Massachusetts. It once contained a viable town, Whitney Place, which was abandoned when the whole Whitney estate was sold to the state in 1912 but became a Civilian Conservation Corps project area in the 1930s. Part of the area is now a water-supply area for the city of Pittsfield, with reservoirs and dams.

N-S

TRAIL DESCRIPTION

0.0	Trail intersects with paved Pittsfield Road, at dirt service road from Pittsfield watershed area. Large A.T. sign marks **northern end of section**. ■ SOUTHBOUND hikers follow dirt service road for a short distance into watershed area. ■ NORTHBOUND hikers cross Pittsfield Road and immediately turn left (see Massachusetts Section 4).	**9.4**
0.1	Trail intersects with dirt service road leading west into Pittsfield watershed area. ■ SOUTHBOUND hikers turn left from road, soon entering **October Mountain State Forest**. ■ NORTHBOUND hikers turn right and follow road east toward Pittsfield Road.	**9.3**
1.5	Cross dirt West Branch Road. Beavers often plug the culvert here and on other streams in this section of Trail, resulting in wet footing in many areas.	**7.9**

S-N

SECTION HIGHLIGHTS

October Mountain Shelter →

Large, 16-person shelter with loft, porch, and privy. Campsites around shelter. Water source is a stream on the A.T. south of shelter. Next shelter: south, 9.3 miles (Upper Goose Pond); north, 9 miles (Kay Wood).

Bald Top →

The summit (no longer bald) that the Trail crosses here, according to V. Collins Chew's book on A.T. geology, *Underfoot,* is a *roche moutonnée* (French for "sheep-shaped rock"), formed when a glacier scraped away one side.

Finerty Pond →

Originally a swamp, dammed up by the Civilian Conservation Corps in the 1930s to provide a water supply for nearby Lee.

| | TRAIL DESCRIPTION | |

2.2	Side trail leads west, near small, intermittent stream, to **October Mountain Shelter**.	**7.2**
3.3	Cross "Gorilla Trail," a motorcycle–ATV (all-terrain vehicle) trail connecting Stanley Road (to east) with County Road (to west).	**6.1**
3.8	Reach overgrown summit of **Bald Top** (2,040 feet).	**5.6**
4.0	Trail intersects County Road and follows it 100 yards to avoid swampy area on south side. County Road leads four miles east to Mass. 8.	**5.4**
5.0	Cross streams, including outlet of Finerty Pond and tributaries of Washington Mountain Brook.	**4.4**
5.8	Reach high point north of **Finerty Pond**.	**3.6**

A.T. bridge over Massachusetts Turnpike

SECTION HIGHLIGHTS

Jacob's Ladder Highway (U.S. 20) →

Built over the Hoosac Range in the early 1900s, one source reports that this 33-mile stretch of U.S. 20 was so named because the dirt road looked like a ladder where rows of dirt known as "thank-you-ma'ams" were built across it, to stop the rain from washing out the track, and where clearings had been cut at which horses and live-stock could rest. The more classical reference, of course, would be to an angel-bedecked ladder to heaven described in the biblical book of Genesis. Just north on the highway toward Beckett is the prestigious Jacob's Pillow Dance center, which stages an international festival each summer.

Southern end of section →

On U.S. 20, five miles east of Lee and Exit 2 of the Massachusetts Turnpike (I-90). Lee (ZIP Code 01238) has many stores and restaurants and bus connections to Boston and Pittsfield. Parking area is 100 yards west.

N-S

TRAIL DESCRIPTION

6.2	Northwest side of Finerty Pond.	**3.0**
6.3	Skirt west side of Finerty Pond.	**2.9**
6.5	South side of Finerty Pond. A.T. crosses an ATV trail.	**2.7**
7.1	Pass overgrown summit of Walling Mountain (2,220 feet)	**2.1**
8.1	Summit of Becket Mountain (2,178 feet). Several concrete footings mark site of a former fire tower. Register box.	**1.1**
8.6	Cross paved Tyne Road (also called Becket Road) near boundary of **October Mountain State Forest**. U.S. 20 is 0.9 mile west; Mass. 8 is 3.5 miles east.	**0.8**
9.2	Pass under powerline.	**0.2**
9.3	Pass blue-blazed trail that leads west to parking area.	**0.1**
9.4	Trail intersects with north side of **U.S. 20, Jacob's Ladder Highway**. Large A.T. sign marks **southern end of section**.	**0.0**

S-N

U.S. 20 (Jacob's Ladder Highway) to Tyringham

8.6 MILES

The Trail in this section crosses the plateau of the Berkshire Highlands, skirting Upper Goose Pond, a dramatic glacial lake that is now part of a National Park Service "natural area." At the southern end of the section, it descends from the highlands into the Hop Brook Valley near Tyringham.

Road approaches—The northern end of this section on U.S. 20 five miles east of Lee has a parking lot 100 yards to the west. Limited parking is available in a roadside lot at the southern end on Tyringham Main Road 0.9 mile east of Tyringham and 4.0 miles east of Lee. Vehicular access also is possible on Goose Pond Road (Tyringham Road), mile 4./4.3 with parking for six cars 50 yards to east, and Webster Road, mile 6.7/1.9, off Tyringham Main Road.

Maps—Refer to ATC's Map 2 for Massachusetts–Connecticut. For area detail, consult the USGS quadrangles listed at the top right of that map.

Shelters and campsites—No camping is permitted, except at Upper Goose Pond Cabin (on a 0.5-mile side trail from mile 1.6/7.0), with tent platforms (open seasonally). Off-season camping is permitted at the cabin, but campfires are not permitted at any time.

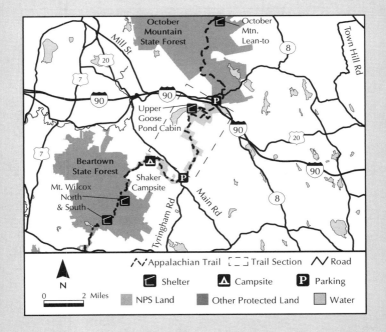

Northern end of section →

On U.S. 20, five miles east of Lee and Exit 2 of the Massachusetts Turnpike (I-90). Lee (ZIP Code 01238), five miles west, has many stores and restaurants and bus connections to Boston and Pittsfield. A parking area is 100 yards west.

Greenwater Pond →

Interstate 90 (the Massachusetts Turnpike) and U.S. 20 (Jacob's Ladder Highway) go through a valley here that formed when Greenwater Brook eroded a marble seam in the Berkshire plateau.

Upper Goose Pond Cabin →

Enclosed cabin, with kitchen, privy, tent platforms, swimming, canoes. Volunteers with the A.T. Committee of the AMC Berkshire Chapter serve as caretakers at the cabin on weekends during spring and fall and all week long during the summer. Camping is not permitted elsewhere along this scenic, crescent-shaped glacial lake, the largest undeveloped body of water in the state. Next shelter: 14.8 miles south (Mt. Wilcox North); north, 9.3 miles (October Mountain).

N-S

| TRAIL DESCRIPTION |

0.0 **Northern end of section.** Trail intersects with south side of U.S. 20 at large A.T. sign.   **8.6**

0.3 Cross stream on high bridge over historical mill site on outlet stream from **Greenwater Pond**.   **8.3**

0.4 Cross Interstate 90 (Massachusetts Turnpike) on twin bridges.   **8.2**

1.0 Reach top of ridge overlooking Interstate 90 (Massachusetts Turnpike) and Upper Goose Pond Natural Area (no camping or campfires allowed). An A.T. register box is located at the ridgetop.   **7.6**

1.6 At foot of ridge, A.T. intersects blue-blazed side trail that leads west in 0.5 mile to **Upper Goose Pond Cabin** and camping area.   **7.0**

Hiker on dock at Upper Goose Pond Cabin

S-N

Goose Pond Road (Tyringham Road) →

Leads west to Goose Pond and three miles to East Lee, or east three miles to Mass. 8. Parking for six cars is 50 yards east of the Trail crossing.

Webster Road →

The Trail crossing here was the site of a thriving community in the 1800s, including two schools. A local legend tells of a self-taught bone-setter named Widow Sweets. Webster Road leads east to Tyringham Main Road.

Southern end of section →

Reached from Lee *via* Tyringham Main Road. Main Road leads west 0.9 mile to Tyringham and its post office (ZIP Code 01264). No food establishments there, and lodging does not cater to hikers. Lee (ZIP Code 01238), four miles west, has many stores, restaurants, and motels; bus connections to Boston and Pittsfield. Limited parking is available in a roadside lot.

N-S

TRAIL DESCRIPTION

1.9	Pass old chimney and plaque identifying the site of former Mohhekennuck fishing and hunting club.	6.7
2.4	Cross inlet of Upper Goose Pond.	6.2
4.1	On telephone-pole bridge at foot of hill, cross outlet marsh of Cooper Brook beaver pond.	4.5
4.2	Trail parallels east side of stone wall. Forest canopy here is white pine.	4.4
4.3	Cross dirt **Goose Pond Road (Tyringham Road)**.	4.3
5.2	Pass unmarked side trail to spring, 0.1 mile west.	3.4
6.1	Unmarked side trail in the midst of hemlock grove gives a view of Knee Deep Pond to west.	2.5
6.7	Cross **Webster Road**.	1.9
6.9	Trail passes through overgrown blueberry fields on top of Baldy Mountain.	1.7
8.6	Trail intersects with north side of Tyringham Main Road, the **southern end of section**.	0.0

S-N

Tyringham to Mass. 23

12.3 MILES

Between Tyringham in the north and Mass. 23 in the south, the Trail follows the southern portion of the Berkshire Highlands (southern Hoosac Range). On the northern end, it traverses farm and hayfields in Tyringham Valley, goes over the historic and geologically significant Tyringham Cobble, passes near Sky Hill, and meanders through Beartown State Forest. On the southern end, it crosses the Ledges, with views to the west of Mt. Everett and the distant Catskills, and skirts Benedict Pond.

Road approaches—The northern end of this section is on Tyringham Main Road 0.9 mile east of Tyringham and 4.0 miles east of Lee; limited parking is avaialble. The southern end is on Mass. 23 four miles east of Great Barrington, with parking at the Trailhead. Vehicular access also can be had from Jerusalem Road (mile 1.1/11.2 0.6 mile from Tyringham) and Blue Hill Road (mile 11.1/1.2; no parking). A parking area at Beartown State Forest is near a blue-blazed trail to the A.T. at Benedict Pond, mile 10.3/2.0.

Maps—Refer to ATC's Map 2 for Massachusetts–Connecticut. For area detail, consult the USGS quadrangles listed at the top right of that map.

Shelters and campsites—Camping is permitted in this section only at the two Mt. Wilcox shelters and the Shaker Campsite tent-platform area.

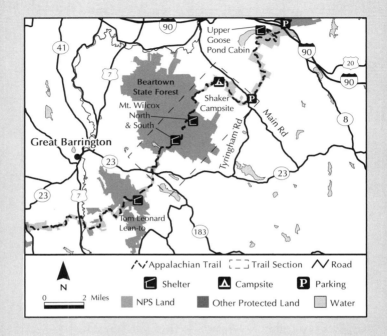

SECTION HIGHLIGHTS

Northern end of section →

On Tyringham Main Road from Lee *via* Mass. 102. Main Road leads west 0.9 mile to Tyringham and its post office (ZIP Code 01264). No food establishments there, and lodging in Tyringham does not cater to hikers. Lee (ZIP Code 01238), four miles west, has many stores, restaurants, and motels; bus connections to Boston and Pittsfield. Limited parking is available at a roadside lot.

Jerusalem Road →

Leads 0.6 mile to Tyringham. Jerusalem was the name of the Shaker community here, established in 1792. At its zenith, it contained more than 200 Shakers housed in three clusters of buildings along Jerusalem Road. Today, five buildings survive in the nearby Fernside community: the Kitchen and Dining Hall, Brothers' and Sisters' House, Elders' House, and the Red Ox Barn.

Tyringham Cobble Reservation →

"Cobble" is a New England term for a rocky hill eroded away from the larger mass of the mountains. Cobble Hill and about 200 acres are owned and managed by a land-conservation organization, the Trustees of Reservations. The A.T. crosses the summit of Cobble Hill, 400 feet above the valley floor. Several rock outcrops offer views of Tyringham Valley, with Hop Brook and the village below. The cobble features wildflowers and other woodland life. Camping and fires are not permitted.

Shaker Campsite →

Camping area with two tent platforms, privy, Trail register. Old cellar holes and wide, carefully made stone walls are all that is left of one part of the Tyringham Shaker community of 1792–1875. The Shakers were a then-radical religious group trying to maintain a utopian Christian community after renouncing property, family, and sexuality. They also were known for elegant, hand-hewn furniture. The water source is a stream crossed by the A.T. just north of the campsite.

N-S	TRAIL DESCRIPTION	
0.0	Trail intersects with south side of Tyringham Main Road, **northern end of section**. Main Road leads west 0.9 mile to Tyringham.	**12.3**
0.1	Cross extensive boardwalk over wet fields in the Hop Brook floodplain.	**12.2**
0.7	Cross buried gas pipeline in wet field at foot of hill.	**11.6**
0.8	Cross intermittent brooks, some *via* small bridges, in hemlock grove.	**11.5**
1.1	Cross **Jerusalem Road**, boundary of **Tyringham Cobble Reservation**.	**11.2**
1.6	A.T. gains the summit of Cobble Hill, with views to the south and east.	**10.7**
2.2	Cross southern boundary of Cobble reservation lands.	**10.1**
2.8	Cross cleared gas pipeline amid a series of fields where the Trail follows hedgerows.	**9.5**
3.1	Short, blue-blazed side trail leads to **Shaker Campsite** at foot of hill.	**9.2**
3.4	Trail crosses dirt Fernside Road.	**8.9**

Tyringham Valley →

Marble, which is more susceptible to erosion than the gneiss of the Berkshire Highlands, has eroded here over the centuries to define the Tyringham Valley.

Beartown State Forest →

The forest spans more than 10,000 acres and includes more than 30 miles of trails. It is so named, according to Katherine Abbott's 1907 work, *Old Paths and Legends of the New England Border*, "because a pioneer of Lee killed bear in the forest depths with a knotted rope's end."

Old A.T. →

The Trail through this section formerly ran from Mt. Wilcox to Tyringham's Jerusalem Road.

Mt. Wilcox North Shelter →

Accommodates eight to ten. The water supply in a nearby brook is prone to go dry in late summer. Privy nearby. Next shelter: south, 2.1 miles (Mt. Wilcox South); north, 14.8 miles (Upper Goose Pond).

Mt. Wilcox South Shelters →

Two shelters. The old, CCC-built shelter accommodates six; the newer shelter (2007), 16. Privy nearby. A spring is on the side of the blue-blazed access trail, 200 feet from the A.T. Another spring is located 100 yards south of the Trail junction, on the eastern side of Trail. Next shelter: south, 5.3 miles (Tom Leonard); north, 2.1 miles (Mt. Wilcox North).

N-S

TRAIL DESCRIPTION

3.9 Trail rises to a white-pine ridge paralleling the **Tyringham Valley**. **8.4**

4.2 Reach stand of hemlock, with view of lower **Tyringham Valley**. **8.1**

4.9 Cross stone walls marking boundary of **Beartown State Forest**. **7.4**

5.9 Near a large swampy area, the A.T. turns sharply through a dry hemlock grove. **6.4**

6.1 Trail crosses a footbridge over outlet from a series of beaver dams. **6.2**

6.6 Trail crosses dirt Beartown Mountain Road, where culvert directs stream to beaver ponds. **5.7**

6.7 A.T. crosses ATV trail ("Airplane Trail") near planted Norway-spruce grove, where old Shaker cellar holes can be found. **5.6**

7.2 Trail joins **old A.T.** on top of ridge for 200 yards where the **Mt. Wilcox North Shelter** is 0.25 mile east on blue-blazed trail. **5.1**

7.8 Trail crosses outlet of another beaver dam and swamp. **4.5**

9.0 Blue-blazed side trail to **Mt. Wilcox South Shelters**. **3.3**

S-N

Benedict Pond →

This glacial pond is now part of Beartown State Forest, with camping (fee; *reservations required*), picnicking, boat launch, swimming area, pay phone, and parking accessible *via* blue-blazed side trail 0.25 mile west along the south shore of the pond.

Blue Hill Road →

No parking is available along this road, which is bordered by private property on both sides. It leads east to Mass. 23, near the Beartown State Forest headquarters.

1995 tornado →

A storm in 1995 damaged this area, felling many oak trees. The oak timber was then logged in a salvage operation managed by the Massachusetts Department of Environmental Management. Compare the way the forest has regenerated here, north of Mass. 23, with the nearby section of the A.T. south of Mass. 23 (in Section Eight), where the tornado devastated a mature white pine forest. That forest, on National Park Service-managed land, was not salvaged.

Southern end of section →

On Mass. 23 four miles east of Great Barrington (ZIP Code 01230), a large town settled in the 1600s, with stores (including supermarkets, coin laundries, a backpacking store, and a cobbler), public accommodations, and restaurants. Bus service is available in Great Barrington, with connections to other towns in Berkshire County. Great Barrington was the first (2009) New England town to be designated an Appalachian Trail Community by ATC in recognition of efforts by the town and local committees to protect and enhance the Trail. Further information about the town and its activities can be found at <www.townofgb.org>. Monterey, a small town with a market and restaurant, is four miles east. Parking available at Trailhead lot.

TRAIL DESCRIPTION

9.1 At powerline, cross old woods road that was the access the Mt. Wilcox fire tower. A radio tower is now situated atop Mt. Wilcox.   **3.2**

9.7 The A.T. follows the Ledges, which afford a view west to East Mountain and Mt. Everett State Forest in the foreground, with the Catskill Mountains in the distance.   **2.6**

9.9 Cross footbridge built from nearby hemlock under which is outflow of a large high elevation beaver swamp.   **2.4**

10.2 Cross abandoned road bridge. Trail turns ninety degrees.   **2.1**

10.3 Follow bog bridges across inlet on east side of **Benedict Pond**.   **2.0**

10.7 A.T. follows a woods road for a short distance as it passes a semicircular charcoal pit.   **1.6**

11.1 Trail crosses boundary of Beartown State Forest at **Blue Hill Road** (Stony Brook Road), at the foot of a cliff with steep rock steps.   **1.2**

11.3 Trail crosses 100 yards of bog bridges and stepping stones through a red maple swamp.   **1.0**

11.9 A.T. intersects with unmarked trail, turns ninety degrees.   **0.4**

12.0 Trail passes through area damaged by a **1995 tornado**.   **0.3**

12.3 **Southern end of section** is in parking lot on north side of Mass. 23 at a large sign.   **0.0**

Mass. 23 to U.S 7

8.4 MILES

The area immediately surrounding Mass. 23 was part of the historic Knox Trail, over which the Colonists took cannons from Lake George, New York, to defend Boston during the Revolutionary War. This section of the A.T. crosses East and June mountains, at the southernmost part of the Berkshire Highlands, and the Housatonic River, the route of which it will generally parallel into central Connecticut. East Mountain offers a scenic ridgewalk through Ice Gulch and a scramble on the steep ledges of its western side.

Road approaches—The northern end of this section is on Mass. 23 four miles east of Great Barrington, with parking at the Trailhead. No parking is available at the southern end on U.S. 7, the major north-south highway through the Berkshires. The Trail also intersects Lake Buel Road (mile 0.9/7.5, with parking at a lot 50 yards north), Homes Road (mile 5.5/2.9) two miles east of U.S. 7 a mile south of Great Barrington, and, at the foot of June Mountain, Boardman Street near Kellogg Road.

Maps—Refer to ATC's Map 2 for Massachusetts–Connecticut. For area detail, consult the USGS quadrangles listed at the top right of that map.

Shelters and Campsites—No camping is permitted in this section, except at Tom Leonard Shelter (mile 2.0/6.4) near Ice Gulch in East Mountain State Forest.

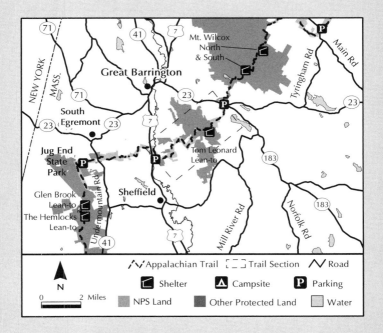

Northern end of section →

On Mass. 23 four miles east of Great Barrington (ZIP Code 01230), a large town settled in the 1600s, with stores (including supermarkets, coin laundries, a backpacking store, and a cobbler), public accommodations, and restaurants. Bus service is available in Great Barrington, with connections to other towns in Berkshire County. Great Barrington was the first (2009) New England town to be designated an Appalachian Trail Community by ATC in recognition of efforts by the town and local committees to protect and enhance the Trail. Further information about the town and its activities can be found at <www.townofgb.org>. Monterey, a small town with a market and restaurant, is four miles east. Parking available at Trailhead lot.

1995 tornado →

This white-pine grove was heavily damaged by a storm in 1995 and can be seen as nature left it, except where the A.T. treadway passes through the timber. Compare the pattern of regrowth to the area north of Mass. 23, managed by the state rather than the National Park Service, where the fallen timber was harvested.

Lake Buel Road →

Leads west (compass-north) two miles to Mass. 23. Great Barrington is three miles west. Parking is available at a lot 50 yards north.

East Mountain State Forest →

The cliffs on the south side of East Mountain overlook Ice Gulch, a ravine where a sharp drop in temperature can usually be observed and ice among boulders at the bottom lingers long after it has melted elsewhere on the mountain. East Mountain is managed by Beartown State Park staff members.

Tom Leonard Shelter →

Named after a former ridgerunner and thru-hiker, the shelter accommodates 16. A nearby tent platform affords an impressive southern view. A privy is nearby. The water source is on a 0.25-mile, blue-blazed trail down to the outlet of Ice Gulch. Next shelter: south, 14.3 miles (Glen Brook); north, 5.3 miles (Mt. Wilcox South).

N-S

TRAIL DESCRIPTION

0.0	**Northern end of section** is in parking lot on north side of Mass. 23 at a large sign.	**8.4**
0.2	Trail passes through area damaged by **1995 tornado**.	**8.2**
0.4	Cross broken cement dam, outlet for swamp that feeds Lake Buel. An old road runs along the south shore of the swamp.	**8.0**
0.5	Cross dirt road.	**7.9**
0.9	Cross paved **Lake Buel Road**.	**7.5**
1.9	Cross border of **East Mountain State Forest** near Ice Gulch, marked by steep cliffs and a view.	**6.5**
2.0	Side trail leads east to **Tom Leonard Shelter**, by intermittent stream crossing (unreliable water source).	**6.4**

Trail bridge north of Homes Road

S-N

SECTION HIGHLIGHTS

Homes Road →

U.S. 7 is two miles west (compass-north). From there, Great Barrington is one mile north.

June Mountain →

Named for Benjamin June, who lived on it. The topography of this section of Trail, across a series of ridges at the edge of the Berkshire Highlands, shows striking and unusual evidence of the action of glaciers scraping and smoothing the bedrock.

Berkshire Highlands →

Between here and the Hoosic River near Cheshire to the north (see Massachusetts Section 3), the A.T. crosses the plateau of the famous Berkshire Highlands (southern Hoosac Range) of western Massachusetts, once a isolated part of the state above the populous river valleys, now a fashionable place to live or vacation. Geologically, the Berkshires comprise a mass of gneiss and schist thrust up over a layer of marble some 400 million years ago as the African continental plate collided with North America.

N-S

	TRAIL DESCRIPTION	

2.5 Pass obscure trail junction near height of land. **5.9**

3.9 Cross obscure woods road that comes steeply up from Brush Hill Road south of the escarpment. **4.5**

4.1 Southernmost end of ridge of East Mountain offers good views of the Housatonic Valley. The A.T. offers a walk along a ledge with good views to the southwest of Mt. Everett, the Taconic Mountains, and the Catskill Mountains farther to the west. **4.3**

4.7 On ridge, cross deep cleft in glacial boulder. An intermittent spring can be found at the bottom of the cleft. **3.7**

4.9 Traverse a steep ledge with good footing. **3.5**

5.1 The A.T. follows an old woods road, the outlines of which are barely discernible on either side of the Trail. **3.3**

5.5 Trail intersects with paved **Homes Road** (Brush Hill Road) at foot of ridge. **2.9**

5.8 Cross intermittent brook midway up June Mountain. **2.6**

6.5 Cross rim of **June Mountain** (1,206 feet), southernmost extent of the **Berkshire Highlands**. **1.9**

7.1 Trail crosses Boardman Street near its intersection with Kellogg Road, at foot of June Mountain. ■ SOUTHBOUND hikers pass along perimeter of farm field before entering woods. **1.3**

S-N

Housatonic River →

The name Housatonic comes from the Mohican Indian word for "place beyond the mountain." It was first explored by European settlers in 1614. Rising near Pittsfield, it flows southward for 148 miles through Massachusetts and Connecticut to Long Island Sound. Historically, river power and river access made this an important farming and industrial area in Massachusetts. It drops 959 feet in its first 119 miles, which makes it popular for canoeing and kayaking to the north of Falls Village, Connecticut, and a source of hydro-electric power to the south. Pollution has been a problem, though, particularly near Pittsfield, where PCB contamination at an EPA "Superfund" site is still being mitigated. Today, the water is relatively clean, but fishing is on a "catch-and-release" basis, and the river should not be used by hikers as a source of drinking water.

Southern end of section →

On U.S. 7, a busy highway as the main north-south route through western Massachusetts and Connecticut. Great Barrington (ZIP Code 01230), a large town, is 1.8 miles west (compass-north), with stores (including supermarkets, coin laundries, an outfitter, and a cobbler), public accommodations and restaurants (see mile 0.0/8.4). Bus service is available in Great Barrington, with connections to other towns in Berkshire County. Sheffield (ZIP Code 01257) is 3.3 miles east, with lodging, restaurants, and markets. No parking is available on U.S. 7.

N-S

TRAIL DESCRIPTION

7.5 Cross **Housatonic River** on Kellogg Road bridge. ■ SOUTH-BOUND hikers turn sharply right. ■ NORTHBOUND hikers turn sharply left. **0.9**

8.3 Cross small footbridge over drainage in middle of agricultural fields along Housatonic River. **0.1**

8.4 **Southern end of section** is at U.S. 7, within sight of farm stands. **0.0**

Housatonic River

S-N

U.S. 7 to Jug End Road

4.5 MILES

The Trail in this section is mostly flat and easy, crossing the Housatonic Valley between the Berkshire Highlands to the northeast and the Taconic mountain range to the southwest. It crosses several roads, passes historic lime kilns, and passes the field where Shays' Rebellion of 1787 was brought to an end.

Road approaches—The northern end of this section is on U.S. 7, the major north-south highway through the Berkshires; no parking available. The southern end on Jug End Road (Curtiss Road) has limited roadside parking. Access also is available from West Road (mile 0.6/3.9), South Egremont Road (mile 1.8/2.7, with a parking lot), and Mass. 41 (mile 3.6/0.9).

Maps—Refer to ATC's Map 3 for Massachusetts–Connecticut. For area detail, consult the USGS quadrangles listed at the top right of that map.

Shelters and campsites—No camping is permitted in this section, which has neither shelters nor campsites.

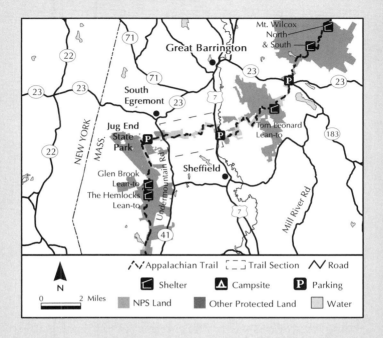

Appalachian Trail · **Trail Section** · **Road** · **Shelter** · **Campsite** · **P Parking** · NPS Land · Other Protected Land · Water

N

0 ___ 2 Miles

SECTION HIGHLIGHTS

Northern end of section →

On U.S. 7, a busy highway as the main north-south route through western Massachuetts and Connecticut. Great Barrington (ZIP Code 01230), a large town, is 1.8 miles west (compass-north), with stores (including supermarkets, coin laundries, an outfitter, and a cobbler), public accommodations and restaurants (see also page 104). Bus service is available in Great Barrington, with connections to other towns in Berkshire County. Sheffield (ZIP Code 01257) is 3.3 miles east, with lodging, restaurants, and markets. No parking is available on U.S. 7.

Housatonic Railroad →

The tracks here were part of the New Haven Railroad's busy Berkshire Division ("The Berk"), running between Bridgeport, Connecticut, and Pittsfield. North of the state line, it was known as the Berkshire Railroad; south of the line, the Housatonic Railroad. Presently, the former Berkshire line is owned by the states of Connecticut and Massachusetts and operated for freight by the Housatonic Railroad. The Trail parallels these tracks again in Connecticut, near Falls Village, but does not cross them.

West Road →

Leads east (compass-south) to South Egremont Road, near U.S. 7. Leads west (compass-north) to Mass. 41, which runs north into Great Barrington and south into Connecticut, paralleling the A.T.

Lime kilns →

Limestone was burned in these kilns to produce lime, a key ingredient in early steel-making.

N-S

| TRAIL DESCRIPTION |

0.0   The **northern end of section** is on U.S. 7. The Trail   **4.5**
crosses an open field south of the highway.

0.1   Cross active railroad tracks of the **Housatonic Railroad**,   **4.4**
with caution signs on both sides.

0.2   Trail crosses a long boardwalk across a swamp.   **4.3**

0.6   Cross **West Road** (also referred to on some maps as West   **3.9**
Sheffield Road) at foot of a low ridge to the south. The
Trail skirts an open field on the south side of the road.

1.3   Trail turns sharply at a gravel driveway. Lime Kiln Road   **3.2**
is 100 yards east, where two historical **lime kilns** can be
seen on the north side of the road.

S-N

SECTION HIGHLIGHTS

Shays' Rebellion Monument →

This western Massachusetts uprising was led by Revolutionary War veteran Daniel Shays (c. 1747–1825) over high taxes and postwar economic woes in late 1786 and early 1787. The "rebels"—essentially an angry mob of farmers and other debtors faced with losing their livelihoods because they did not have the gold and silver demanded as payment—closed courts from Springfield west to prevent foreclosures against their property. More than 1,000 of Shays' followers marched on a major arsenal in Springfield but were turned away and later pursued and defeated by a private militia hired by urban creditors and, later, state militia forces. A final battle took place in February 1787 near the marker here on the "Sheffield Plain," with many of the rebels captured. Shays was sentenced to death for his part in the uprising but escaped to Vermont and, later, New York. He was eventually pardoned and received a veteran's pension. The rebellion and response to it prompted General George Washington, from retirement, to speak out for a stronger central government and soon generated calls that led to the Constitutional Convention in May 1787.

South Egremont Road →

Leads west two miles to village of South Egremont and east to U.S. 7. Parking is available in a roadside lot.

	TRAIL DESCRIPTION	

1.8	Trail passes **Shays' Rebellion Monument** on the north side of **South Egremont Road** (Sheffield Road), with a parking lot on the south side of the Trail at the road crossing.	2.7
2.0	Cross Hubbard Brook on short boardwalk and bridge.	2.5
2.8	Cross bog bridges on north side of a small ridge, south of an expanse of swampy ground.	1.7
3.2	A.T. turns and follows an old woods road along a narrow ridge.	1.3
3.4	Cross bog bridges over intermittent farm brook.	1.1

Shays' Rebellion Monument

SECTION HIGHLIGHTS

Mass. 41 →

Leads 1.2 miles west to village of South Egremont (ZIP Code 01258), where food, lodging, and groceries can be found. No parking is available at the crossing.

April Hill Farm →

An intact, Colonial-era (1742), Appalachian Trail Conservancy property also protected through easements held by the National Park Service and state agencies. Now called the Kellogg Conservation Center, it houses the ATC's New England regional office. AMC also has a regional office here. In 2004, longtime benefactor Mary-Margaret Kellogg donated this historic home and 95-acre farm as an additional means to support the mission of the Conservancy and ensure that her beloved landscape will be available for the enjoyment of generations to come.

Southern end of section →

On Jug End Road (Curtiss Road), which intersects to the east with Mass. 41, the highway between the village of South Egremont (ZIP Code 01258) and the Connecticut town of Salisbury (the southern end of Connecticut Section One). On the south side of the road is a small pull-off for two to three cars.

N-S

TRAIL DESCRIPTION

3.6   Cross **Mass. 41** in the middle of **April Hill Farm**, now ATC's Kellogg Conservation Center.   **0.9**

4.0   A mature white-pine forest surrounds the Trail for 0.4 mile.   **0.5**

4.5   The **southern end of section** is found at Jug End Road. .A spring on the south side of the road is 0.25 mile farther east.   **0.0**

S-N

Jug End Road to Sages Ravine

9.5 MILES

The southernmost section of the A.T. in Massachusetts stretches between the foot of the Taconic Range and the Connecticut line, which it approaches north of Bear Mountain. It is a rugged section, often running along glacier-scoured ridgecrest rocks, and few sections of similar mileage can match it for views. The A.T. along the top of the precipices of the Race Mountain escarpment has magnificent views. Throughout the section, the Trail passes through open woodlands of hardwoods and conifers, heavily populated with laurel and blueberry shrubs. Rattlesnakes (a protected species here) are seen occasionally in this section. Unlike most sections of the Trail in Massachusetts, the southern section is not accessible by vehicle, except in the summer by the Mt. Everett day-use access road.

Road approaches—The northern end of this section on Jug End Road (Curtiss Road) has limited roadside parking. The southern end is accessible only by the Trail.

Maps—Refer to ATC's Map 3 for Massachusetts–Connecticut. For area detail, consult the USGS quadrangles listed at the top right of that map.

Shelters and campsites—This section has two shelters: Glen Brook (mile 3.4/6.1) and Hemlocks (mile 3.5/6.0), both on side trails. Laurel Ridge Campsite (mile mile 8.3/1.2) has tent pads, tent platforms, and a privy, and, at Sages Ravine, about 0.6 mile south of the southern end of the section, there is a campsite with a caretaker. A half-mile off the Trail at mile 5.3/4.2, designated campsites with tent platforms, privies, and water are located at Race Brook Falls.

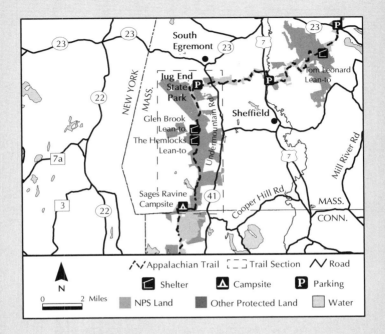

Appalachian Trail · Trail Section · Road
Shelter · Campsite · P Parking
NPS Land · Other Protected Land · Water

0 — 2 Miles

N

SECTION HIGHLIGHTS

Northern end of section →

On Jug End Road (Curtiss Road), which intersects to the east with Mass. 41 (Salisbury Road), the highway between the village of South Egremont (ZIP Code 01258) and the Connecticut town of Salisbury (at the southern end of Connecticut Section One). On the south side of the road is a small pull-off for two to three vehicles.

Taconic Range →

The Taconics get their name from the Indian word *Taghkonic*, thought to derive from the Algonkian word for "tree" or "forest."

Jug End →

Jug End Mountain (1,750 feet) stands on the northern end of the Mt. Everett massif in the Taconics. The ledges here are of schist. The name, an Anglicization of the German *Jungend*, recalls a youth camp on the western side of the mountain.

Elbow Trail →

Blazed blue, this trail descends 1.5 miles to the Berkshire School on Mass. 41.

Glen Brook Shelter →

This older shelter accommodates four, but two tent platforms and an extensive tenting area are adjacent. A creek and a privy are nearby. Next shelter: south, 0.1 mile (Hemlocks); north, 14.3 miles (Tom Leonard).

Hemlocks Shelter →

This shelter, 0.1 mile from the A.T. on the eastern side, accommodates 16. A privy and limited tentsites are nearby. Next shelter: south, 8.8 miles (Brassie Brook); north, 0.1 mile (Glen Brook).

N-S

TRAIL DESCRIPTION

0.0 The **northern end of section** is at Jug End Road, at the foot of Jug End, a steep, rocky summit of the **Taconic Range**. A spring, located on the same side of the road, is 0.25 mile farther east. **9.5**

0.7 Cross exposed rock faces above steep section on the north side of Jug End. *Use extra caution in wet conditions.* **8.8**

1.1 Rocky summit of **Jug End**, with good views to north and east, including the expanse of the Berkshire Highlands (southern Hoosac Range) and extending all the way to Mt. Greylock, the state's highest point, near the Vermont line. **8.4**

2.3 Trail crosses three small summits over a 0.75-mile stretch, the largest one being Mt. Bushnell (1,834 feet). **7.2**

2.8 Blue-blazed **Elbow Trail** intersects on the east side of Trail at a sharp bend in the Trail. The Elbow Trail descends east to Berkshire School on Mass. 41. **6.7**

2.9 An old side trail from the Jug End resort (acreage now jointly owned by the state forest and parks and the fish and wildlife divisions) is barely discernible to the west across a small stream. **6.6**

3.4 Side trail to **Glen Brook Shelter** intersects on the east side of A.T. **6.1**

3.5 Cross Glen Brook (water supply for shelter if treated). Side trail east to **Hemlocks Shelter** on the south side of the brook. **6.0**

SECTION HIGHLIGHTS

Guilder Pond Picnic Area →

A day-use picnic area includes a privy and picnic tables, but no swimming, camping, or fishing is permitted. Seasonal access is available from Washington Road to the west.

Mt. Everett →

The "Dome of the Taconics," at 2,602 feet. The summit affords limited views, but, as the A.T. ascends the northern side, vistas to the north, east, and south open up. Mt. Everett's origins go back to the mountain-building episode known as the Taconic orogeny about 400 million years ago: a major geological event that built much of the Appalachian mountain chain. On Mt. Everett itself, you can see evidence of something much more recent, geologically speaking— the Ice Age. The rocks atop Mt. Everett were scraped and scoured by glaciers moving north to south until about 10,000 years ago, when the ice melted. The mountain is now the centerpiece of the Mt. Everett State Reservation.

Race Brook Falls Trail →

Descends two miles to the east to Mass. 41 from the saddle between Mt. Everett and Mt. Race, past several waterfalls, one of which is 100 feet high. Parking space is available on Mass. 41.

Campsite →

Accessible *via* Race Brook Falls Trail, 0.5 mile down east of the A.T. Site includes wooden tent platforms and privy.

N-S

	TRAIL DESCRIPTION	

3.8   Blue-blazed side trail to Guilder Pond (2,042 feet), high-   **5.7**
est natural freshwater pond in Massachusetts, intersects
on the west side of the A.T.

3.9   The Trail passes day-use-only **Guilder Pond Picnic Area**   **5.6**
in the Mt. Everett State Reservation.

4.0   Cross summit road.   **5.5**

4.6   Summit of **Mt. Everett** (2,602 feet).   **4.9**

5.3   A.T. descends steeply on slippery bedrock and enters the   **4.2**
saddle between Mt. Race and Mt. Everett. Blue-blazed
Race Brook Falls Trail intersects on east side. A designated **campsite** can be found in 0.5 mile, and this trail
continues 1.5 miles farther to Mass. 41.

Glen Brook Shelter

S-N

SECTION HIGHLIGHTS

Mt. Race →

The open summit enables a 360-degree view of the Taconics, Monument Mountain, Mt. Greylock (40 miles away), and nearby Mt. Everett in the north to Connecticut's Bear Mountain in the south; Brace Mountain, Mt. Frissell, Alander Mountain, Mt. Darby, and the Catskills in New York to the west; and East and Warner mountains to the east, along with the Housatonic Valley. South of the summit, the A.T. skirts close to the edge of a cliff offering more views to the east.

Laurel Ridge Campsite →

Wooden tent platforms and earthen tent pads, with a privy just east of the A.T. The water source is a spring south of the campsite. No fires are permitted at this site.

Southern end of section →

The southern end of this section can be reached only by the A.T. itself, with the closest A.T. Trailhead 7.4 miles south along the Trail at the southern end of Connecticut Section 1. The Undermountain Trail, in Connecticut, 2.3 miles south of the section's southern end, leads to a heavily used blue-blazed trailhead on Conn. 41 (Undermountain Road).

N-S

TRAIL DESCRIPTION

6.4 Summit of Race Mountain. Trail traverses an open ledge **3.1**
with fine views into the Housatonic Valley.

6.6 The Trail near here follows close to the edge of the escarp- **2.9**
ment.

8.1 Cross Bear Rock Stream. **1.4**

8.3 **Laurel Ridge Campsite** is on the west side of the Trail, **1.2**
near a spring. Tent platforms, tents pads, and a privy. *Fires
are not permitted at this campsite.*

9.5 **Southern end of section** is at Sawmill Brook (in Sages **0.0**
Ravine), the dividing point of maintenance responsibility
between the Berkshire and Connecticut chapters of the
Appalachian Mountain Club. There is no Trailhead here
nor is there a trail down to Conn. 41 from Sages Ravine;
attempts to bushwhack down have often led to accidents
and very expensive rescues. Massachusetts State Forest
and Parks land extends about a Trail-mile farther south
before the footpath crosses into Connecticut. Sages Ravine
Brook Campsite is located in Connecticut Section One,
just up the ravine, with tent platforms and a privy available.

S-N

Connecticut

The most dominant geographical features of the Trail in Connecticut are the Taconic Range, which the Trail follows in the northern part of the state, and the Housatonic River, the valley of which the Trail follows or parallels for most of its passage here. In general, Connecticut offers a mix of easy and moderate hiking, including a lengthy river walk, and one short section of Trail near Falls Village that is accessible to wheelchairs. But, especially in the Taconics and on the high ledges west of Kent, it also features some steep and difficult sections. ***No campfires are permitted along the Appalachian Trail in Connecticut***.

When the Trail was first planned, some early builders advocated having it skip Connecticut entirely, in favor of a route up through New

York, east of the Hudson. Another suggestion would have kept the Trail on the west side of the Housatonic (its present location). A route through the town of Cornwall finally was selected, built, and largely maintained for 20 years by local Trail pioneer Nestell Kip "Ned" Anderson in 1932. It remained there, with some modifications, until 1988. Most of the old "eastern route" of the A.T. is now part of the Blue Trail System of the Connecticut Forest and Park Association and is known as the Mohawk Trail.

Much of the Trail in Connecticut follows the valley of the Housatonic River, an area rich in history. Although industry is largely gone from the region today, there are many ruins and remnants of the time when the river was a bustling center of early New England industrial activity and projected activity.

View from St. Johns Ledges

Sages Ravine to Conn. 41

7.4 MILES

The northernmost section of the A.T. in Connecticut begins high on the Taconic mountain range and passes through an area of historical interest. Bear Mountain, near the northern end of the section, offers good views of the entire Taconic Range, in addition to the Berkshire Highlands of Massachusetts, to the north. The Trail also crosses Lions Head, with views to the east, before descending to the valley of Salisbury. The ascents here are more strenuous than in other sections of Connecticut but are moderate compared to the Appalachian Trail north of Massachusetts.

Road approaches—The northern end of this section is accessible only by the Trail. The southern end on Conn. 41 (Undermountain Road) has ample parking space between two private residences (please do not approach them).

Maps—Refer to ATC's Map 3 for Massachusetts–Connecticut. For area detail, consult the USGS quadrangles listed at the top right of that map.

Shelters and campsites—No camping is permitted in this section, except at designated campsites or shelters. Those include Sages Ravine Brook (mile 0.6/6.8), Brassie Brook (mile 2.6/4.6), Ball Brook (mile 3.4/4.0), and Riga (mile 4.0/3.4) campsites, and Brassie Brook (mile 2.8/4.6) and Riga (mile 4.0/3.4) shelters. Group camping is permitted at Ball Brook and near the Paradise Lane Trail (1.1 miles east from its A.T. intersection at mile 2.3/5.1).

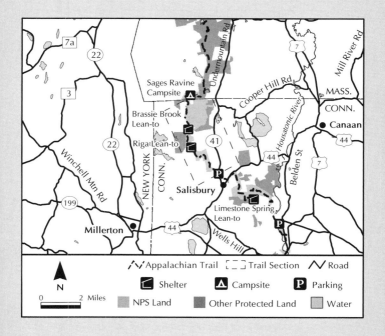

Appalachian Trail   Trail Section   Road

Shelter   Campsite   Parking

NPS Land   Other Protected Land   Water

Northern end of section →

The northern end of this section can be reached only by the A.T. itself, with the nearest northbound A.T. Trailhead 9.5 miles away, at Jug End Road in Massachusetts (see Massachusetts Section Ten). Blue-blazed Race Brook Trail, 4.2 miles north of Sages Ravine, leads to Mass. 41. Undermountain Trail, 2.3 miles south of the section's northern end, leads to a heavily used blue-blazed trailhead on Conn. 41 (Undermountain Road). From the west side of the ridge,

Sages Ravine Brook Campsite →

Designated camping area on northern side of Sawmill Brook in Sages Ravine. Caretaker on duty in summer months. Tent platforms and privy available. Spring flows except in very dry seasons. No fires allowed at any time.

N-S

TRAIL DESCRIPTION

0.0 **Northern end of section is** Sawmill Brook (Sages Ravine Brook), which marks the historic division of Trail-management responsibility between the Connecticut and Berkshire chapters of the Appalachian Mountain Club. There is no trail down to Conn. 41 from Sages Ravine; attempts to bushwhack down have often resulted in accidents and very expensive rescues.   **7.5**

0.6 **Sages Ravine Brook Campsite**. Large trees and waterfalls in this ravine, interspersed by quiet pools, make this an especially attractive and popular section of the Trail.   **6.8**

Sages Ravine brook

S-N

Paradise Lane Trail →

Built by AMC in 1954, skirts Bear Mountain and leads to the Paradise Lane group camping area, which has an open-sided "chum" privy. No fires allowed at the camping area. At 2.1 miles, it meets the Undermountain Trail, which leads 1.1 miles east to Conn. 41 north of Salisbury. In bad weather, these two trails can be used to bypass the A.T. route on the northern side of Bear Mountain, which is very steep and requires much caution, especially in wet or icy conditions.

Bear Mountain →

The highest mountain entirely within Connecticut, although not the state's highest point. It offers a view of the Housatonic Valley to the east and south and the Berkshires to the north. To the east, in the valley, are the Twin Lakes, four miles away. Beyond the lakes is Canaan Mountain and beyond that the tower on Haystack Mountain in Norfolk. To the north, the view extends past Mt. Everett, the "Dome of the Taconics," all the way to Mt. Greylock, 50 miles away and the highest mountain in Massachusetts. To the west, across the "Riga Plateau" and the Harlem Valley, the view extends to the Catskill Mountains of New York. The state's highest point, at 2,380 feet, is on the south shoulder of Mt. Frissell, the summit of which is in Massachusetts. The cairn on top of Bear Mountain is what remains of a tower built in 1885 by Robbins Battell of Norfolk. Bear Mountain was deeded to the state by the estate of Ellen Battell Stoeckel in 1952. Battell, who paid for the tower (which was actually built by Owen Travis, a Salisbury mason), leased five acres on the summit for 999 years, in 1885, from the Millerton Iron Company. His tower stood unharmed 80 years but has since been vandalized and rebuilt three times. It is now only one-third its former height. Nevertheless, it is easy to climb and provides an excellent perch from which to observe the surrounding landscape.

N-S

TRAIL DESCRIPTION

0.7 **Paradise Lane Trail** intersects above the ravine on the east side of Trail and links to the Undermountain Trail, leading down from the mountain. A group camping area is east of the intersection with the A.T. It is more easily reached by way of the Undermountain Trail. **6.7**

1.4 Cross summit of **Bear Mountain** (2,316 feet). Stone cairn marks what was once thought to be the highest point in Connecticut. Trail on south side of Bear Mountain is less steep than the northern side and offers many views, as well as stony ledges and scrub oak. **6.0**

2.0 Trail turns sharply below Bear Mountain. **5.5**

View of Mt. Everett from Bear Mountain

S-N

Charcoal road →

Charcoal that fed a Revolutionary War-era blast furnace in Salisbury was hauled down roads through these hills. Many charcoal pits can be seen throughout the area. These are actually level circles of land about 20 feet in diameter, often higher than the surrounding land, on which piles of logs were placed and converted into charcoal by controlled burning. They are often recognized today by blackened soil. A nineteenth-century village grew up around the furnace at Forge Pond, west of the Trail. It had enough souls to support a seventy-one-pupil school, a four-clerk department store, and a ballroom. Today, the settlement consists of only a few summer camps, and the dirt roads are not plowed in winter. The A.T. follows an old road for nearly two miles between Riga Shelter and Bear Mountain.

Brassie Brook Camping Area and Shelter →

Formerly called Bond Shelter, it accommodates six. Built by Appalachian Mountain Club and CETA in 1980. Water is at stream north of the blue-blazed trail to the shelter. Privy and picnic table nearby, with ample space for tents. No fires allowed. Next shelter: south, 1.2 miles (Riga); north, 8.8 miles (Hemlocks).

Ball Brook Campsite →

No facilities at campsite; a privy is located at the group camping area. No fires allowed.

Riga Shelter and Camping Area →

Built in 1990 by AMC; accommodates six. Privy nearby. Spring near blue-blazed trail, with second water source along side trail, may go dry during droughts. No fires allowed. Next shelter: south, 8.0 miles (Limestone Spring); north, 1.2 miles (Brassie Brook). To the west is the Riga Plateau, once home to a significant post-Revolutionary War blast furnace. The plateau was sold to three families who in 1923 formed the Mt. Riga Corporation. It, in turn, sold 125 acres to the AMC and 1,300 acres to the National Park Service for the A.T. but retains more than 4,000 acres and two lakes.

N-S

TRAIL DESCRIPTION

2.1	Bear Mountain Road, an old **charcoal road** not passable by car, intersects in clearing below Bear Mountain from west side of Trail.	**5.4**
2.3	"Riga Junction"—the Trail intersects with Undermountain Trail, which leads east 1.1 miles to **Paradise Lane Trail** and group camping area, and 1.9 miles to Conn. 41, at the most popular trailhead in Connecticut.	**5.1**
2.8	Cross Brassie Brook. **Brassie Brook Camping Area and Shelter** are 75 yards east from A.T. along a blue-blazed trail just south of the brook crossing.	**4.6**
3.4	Cross Ball Brook. **Ball Brook Campsite** is north of brook; group camping area is south of brook. Both are on east side of trail.	**4.0**
4.0	**Riga Shelter and Camping Area** is on blue-blazed trail east of A.T.	**3.4**
4.2	Blue-blazed trail leading onto private property intersects on west side of A.T.	**3.2**
4.4	Trail reaches level area on ridge below Lions Head.	**3.0**

S-N

SECTION HIGHLIGHTS

Lions Head →

From the summit, the Twin Lakes, visible in the valley four miles east, are the most prominent feature. Beyond the lakes are Canaan and Prospect mountains and, beyond that, the tower on Haystack Mountain in Norfolk.

Taconic Range →

Geologists call a mountain-building episode that occurred some 400 million years ago the "Taconic Orogeny." In this major geological event, which built much of the Appalachians, volcanic sediment was shoved westward. The Taconics show what is left after 400 million years of erosion. According to V. Collins Chew, the Taconics are "eroded remnants of a great mass of sediments that washed from volcanic islands, turned to schist, and were shoved or slid from far to the east to their present resting place on top of the marble and more locally derived schist. Rock moved in great slices, somewhat like shingles sliding over one another."

Bypass trail →

To west 0.1 mile of the two summits of Lions Head; recommended for use in bad weather to avoid the rocky and steep climb or descent along the ledges of Lions Head.

Lions Head Trail →

Former A.T. route leads 0.4 mile south across private property to Bunker Hill Road, with parking.

Southern end of section →

On Conn. 41 (Undermountain Road). The classic New England village of Salisbury (ZIP Code 06068) is 0.8 mile south, at intersection of U.S. 44 and Conn. 41. Groceries, restaurants, lodging, and stores are available. Lakeville is two miles south of Salisbury and has a coin laundry, hardware store, pizza restaurant, bank, doctor, and dentist. Mouldering privy and bulletin board at Trailhead. Ample parking space is available between two private residences, so please do not approach them. No camping permitted at Trailhead.

N-S

TRAIL DESCRIPTION

4.6 North outlook of **Lions Head**, with views to the north of Bear Mountain and, in the distance, Mt. Greylock in northern Massachusetts. Blue-blazed **bypass trail** intersects on west side. **2.8**

4.7 Summit of **Lions Head** (1,738 feet) and ridgeline of the **Taconic Range**, with view to east of Sheffield and Salisbury. **2.7**

4.8 Blue-blazed **bypass trail** intersects on west side, below summit of Lions Head. **2.6**

4.9 Blue-blazed **Lions Head Trail** intersects on west side. Trail turns sharply. **2.5**

5.0 Trail passes through birch forest, with heavy fern undergrowth during summer months. **2.4**

5.2 Cross old charcoal road. **2.2**

5.3 Pass old stone farm wall. **2.1**

5.6 Cross small stream, usually a dependable source of water. **1.8**

6.7 Pass trail sometimes used by local motorcyclists. Sandy and gravelly soil here is the only clue that the Trail crosses a moraine—rock and gravel deposited by an Ice Age glacier—for the mile above the Sheffield–Salisbury valley. **0.7**

7.2 Side trail leads east to spring in 270 feet. **0.2**

7.4 **Southern end of section** is on Conn. 41 (Undermountain Road). **0.0**

S-N

Conn. 41 to Conn. 112

10.8 MILES

The northern end of the section is north of the village of Salisbury, which the Trail skirts. South of U.S. 44, the Trail ascends a section with good views, passes through the town park on the plateau below the summit of Barrack Matiff (also called "Wetauwanchu Mountain") and Prospect Mountain. Between Prospect Mountain and Sharon Mountain, just south of the end of the section, it follows the Housatonic Valley past the town of Falls Village. This section is rich in history, especially at the Housatonic River end. Near Falls Village are many remnants and ruins from the valley's industrial past. A hydroelectric plant at Falls Village still operates today. The southern end of the section is at the Ethan Allen Highway (U.S. 7), named for the Vermont patriot who was a native of Litchfield (and at one time active in the Salisbury iron industry).

Road approaches—The northern end of this section on Conn. 41 (Undermountain Road) has ample parking space between two private residences (please do not approach them). The southern end is at the intersection of U.S. 7 and Conn. 112 two miles south of Falls Village; parking is available in a triangle north of Conn. 112. At the crossing of U.S. 44 (mile 0.7/10.1), park on the grass between the road and a stone wall. Vehicular access also is possible along Lower Cobble Road (mile 0.4/10.4), Housatonic River Road (mile 7.6/3.2) in Falls Village and Warren Turnpike (mile 9.3/1.5).

Maps—Refer to ATC's Map 3 for Massachusetts–Connecticut. For area detail, consult the USGS quadrangles listed at the top right of that map.

Shelters and campsites—No camping is permitted in this section, except at the one shelter, Limestone Spring (mile 4.1/6.7), between Salisbury and Falls Village on a side trail.

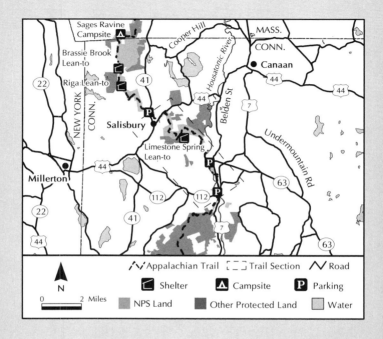

Northern end of section →

On Conn. 41 (Undermountain Road). Parking lot is 150 feet north of where Trail crosses Conn. 41. The quintessential New England village of Salisbury (ZIP Code 06068) is 0.8 mile south, at intersection of U.S. 44 and Conn. 41. Groceries, restaurants, lodging, and stores are available. Lakeville is two miles south of Salisbury. Ample parking space is available at the Trailhead lot between the two private residences, so please do not approach them. The one to the south once belonged to the AMC and was known as the "Undermountain House," which also served as the Appalachian Mountain Club's regional office in southern New England. A mouldering privy and bulletin board are at the Trailhead, but no camping is permitted.

Central New England Railroad →

The railroad was chartered in 1872. At one time, as many as 10 trains a day followed this route between Hartford and Poughkeepsie, New York. Most recently, it was part of the Penn Central; the tracks here last carried freight traffic in 1966.

Barrack Matiff →

The Trail climbs (or descends) sharply between this mountain and U.S. 44. A town park is on top of the plateau. The origin of the name is not really known. A theory that the name is a corruption of some obsolete Dutch words is a matter of debate, even though the earliest settlers in Salisbury were Dutch. Modern topographical maps refer to the mountain as "Wetauwanchu," and there were Indian caves on the western base of the mountain. Edgar Heermance, who wrote the first guidebook, and many guidebook editors after him misnamed it "Barkmeteth Ridge," but Barrack Matiff it is and always has been to the people of Salisbury.

N-S

TRAIL DESCRIPTION

0.0   **Northern end of section** on west side of Conn. 41.   **10.8**

0.4   Trail intersects with paved Lower Cobble Road. ■ SOUTH-   **10.4**
BOUND hikers road-walk along Lower Cobble Road.
■ NORTHBOUND hikers leave Lower Cobble Road on north-
ern side and enter field.

0.6   Trail turns 90 degrees where Lower Cobble Road inter-   **10.3**
sects with U.S. 44. Tracks of the **Central New England
Railroad** once crossed here. ■ SOUTHBOUND hikers follow
U.S. 44 east. ■ NORTHBOUND hikers cross U.S. 44 and
road-walk along Lower Cobble Road.

0.7   Trail intersects U.S. 44. ■ SOUTHBOUND hikers pass through   **10.1**
gap in stone wall to follow field before beginning a series
of switchbacks up **Barrack Matiff** (Wetauwanchu Mountain). ■ NORTHBOUND hikers pass through gap in wall and
follow U.S. 44 toward Salisbury, half a mile west.

1.5   Plateau of **Barrack Matiff** (Wetauwanchu Mountain).   **9.3**

2.6   Cross right-of-way for buried cable laid in 1960s as part   **8.2**
of a coast-to-coast communications system for national
defense; it is no longer used for that purpose. Trail through
here follows abandoned Town Road (not on map), which
once connected Sugar Hill Road and Prospect Mountain
roads.

S-N

SECTION HIGHLIGHTS

Giant's Thumb →

This spot on Raccoon Hill also has some interesting (but far-fetched) theories as to the origin of its name. One is that it was a Viking stone. It is an outcropping, or cobble, around which the ground has eroded.

Rand's View →

Named for the family that owned Hamlet Hill Farm for many years, it offers one of the best viewpoints on the Trail. Panoramic views of the Taconic range, from Bear Mountain to Jug End in Massachusetts, can be had. Following the Trail north along that range will eventually lead hikers to Mt. Greylock, which on clear days can be seen in the distance, 50 miles away, from Rand's View.

Limestone Spring Shelter →

Reached *via* steep 0.5-mile, blue-blazed trail built by AMC in 1986, this shelter accommodates six. Water source, from which the shelter gets its name, is behind it; stream flows from a small limestone cave. Next shelter: south, 12.8 miles (Pine Swamp Brook); north, 8 miles (Riga).

Prospect Mountain →

From the summit, the view extends across the Housatonic Valley to Canaan Mountain, another good hiking area, and takes in the limestone quarries for which Canaan is noted. The rock of this plateau is schist, originally mud from the continental shelf before the plates began colliding 500 million years ago. The sparkles of mica and other shiny rocks in the schist testify to the heat that was generated by the continental collision.

TRAIL DESCRIPTION

Rand's View

3.2 Reach "Billy's View," named after a member of the family that once owned this property, which has since been given to the Salisbury Association. Views to the south over the Salmon Kill Valley. **7.6**

3.6 Cross **Giant's Thumb** rock formation on Raccoon Hill. **7.2**

4.0 Pass **Rand's View**, one of the best views on the A.T. **6.8**

4.1 Blue-blazed side trail to **Limestone Spring Shelter** intersects on west side. A.T. turns 90 degrees at the intersection with the side trail. **6.7**

4.8 Summit of **Prospect Mountain** (1,475 feet). ■ Southbound hikers begin a long descent to the Housatonic River. **6.0**

7.1 Pass seasonal spring on east side of Trail. **3.7**

SECTION HIGHLIGHTS

Great Falls →

These can be spectacular in times of high water but are usually dry in summer. The valley here is mostly underlain by marble, but the falls, like the mountains to their west, are over schist. Rocks along the river are mostly glacial debris. Before the nearby dam was built, a railroad bridge spanned the river here, and, just north of the dam, the foundations of Ames Iron Works are still visible. Parking is readily available on Housatonic River Road.

Iron bridge →

Built about 1870 to replace a 125-year-old wooden bridge. A bridge like it in Pennsylvania was moved in 1984 and reassembled to carry the Appalachian Trail across Swatara Creek. West of the river is an interpretive trail (a 15-minute walk) tracing the industrial history of the area.

Hydroelectric plant →

Northeast Utilities, which operates the plant, offers a brochure that provides information about the dam and directions for a self-guided tour of the area east of the river; it provides details about nineteenth-century plans for industrial development here. Water and a cold shower are available outside the vine-covered building near the transformer.

Canal →

The massive stone wall on the east side of the river from Iron Bridge was built in 1851 as part of a canal system, which was supposed to make Falls Village—then still part of what is now North Canaan—into a large industrial city, modeled after Holyoke, Massachusetts. Unbelievably, the canal leaked because the engineers had neglected to use mortar! The old canal is still unused, but, in 1912, the Connecticut Power Company built a new one. Most of the machinery in the plant dates from that year but has been meticulously maintained. In 1989, a section of the upper canal, near the dam, gave way during a storm, disrupting service for a year.

TRAIL DESCRIPTION

Taconic Range from field near Prospect Mountain

7.6 Trail crosses Housatonic River Road. To east, on the Housatonic River, is **Great Falls**. ■ Southbound hikers follow the river. ■ Northbound hikers cross road and begin climb of Prospect Mountain. **3.2**

8.2 Cross Housatonic River on **iron bridge**. ■ Southbound hikers follow Trail on road between **hydroelectric plant** and old **canal**. ■ Northbound hikers follow west bank of Housatonic River toward Great Falls. **2.6**

River Trail →
Formerly a blue-blazed side trail, AMC and local volunteers developed this to accommodate visitors with disabilities. Part of it follows a nineteenth-century harness racing track. Historic sites along the way are marked.

Housatonic Railroad →
Running between Bridgeport, Connecticut, and Pittsfield, Massachusetts, the New Haven Railroad carried passengers and freight along this line from 1836 to 1972. The Housatonic Railroad was reestablished in 1984 as a private railroad on a state-owned right-of-way and used initially as a scenic railroad; more recently, it has been used exclusively to haul freight.

Housatonic Valley Regional High School →
First regional high school in New England, opened in 1939.

Mohawk Trail →
This trail, the route of the A.T. until 1988, diverges here, crossing U.S. 7 and ascending Barrack Mountain as part of the Blue Trail system of the Connecticut Forest and Park Association. It rejoins the A.T. twenty-four miles south, near Cornwall Bridge. A loop of 37.2 miles is possible on the two trails. (See pages 177–181 for complete trail descriptions.)

Southern end of section →
On U.S. 7 near intersection with Conn. 112. Parking available in triangle north of Conn. 112. Falls Village (ZIP Code 06031) is two miles north *via* U.S 7. Cornwall is five miles south *via* U.S. 7.

N-S

TRAIL DESCRIPTION

8.3 Road intersects with wheelchair-accessible **River Trail.** ■ SOUTHBOUND hikers follow A.T. along east bank of the Housatonic River. ■ NORTHBOUNDERS follow road between hydroelectric plant and old canal. **2.5**

9.3 Cross Warren Turnpike. ■ SOUTHBOUNDERS follow close to tracks of active **Housatonic Railroad.** ■ NORTHBOUNDERS follow the River Trail. **1.5**

10.1 Trail follows Warren Turnpike past **Housatonic Valley Regional High School**. Just north of school along A.T. is northern terminus of **Mohawk Trail** (route of the A.T. until 1988), on east side of Warren Turnpike. **0.7**

10.2 Cross Housatonic River on U.S. 7. ■ SOUTHBOUND hikers follow highway south for 100 yards, then enter woods, and skirt cornfield on berm close to river. ■ NORTHBOUND hikers leave woods, cross bridge, follow highway north for 100 yards, and follow Warren Turnpike toward school. **0.6**

10.8 **Southern end of section** is near junction of U.S. 7 and Conn. 112. ■ NORTHBOUND hikers cross U.S. 7 and skirt cornfield on berm close to Housatonic River. **0.0**

S-N

Conn. 112 to Conn. 4

11.5 MILES

The Trail in this section climbs Sharon Mountain, a name given to an area rather than a specific peak. The northernmost 10 miles of the section are mostly in the Housatonic State Forest, where hunting is permitted in season. It offers some excellent views of the Housatonic Valley. Just before the southern end of the section, the Trail crosses Old Sharon Road, once a major connecting route in the area. At the southern end, the Trail descends to and crosses beautiful Guinea Brook just before reaching Conn. 4, the end of the section. All this section was the subject of a major A.T. relocation. First proposed during the early days of the Trail, it was not built until 56 years after the Trail was first completed through the area. The current route was completed in 1988, and the old route is now known as the Mohawk Trail.

Road approaches—The northern end of this section is at the intersection of U.S. 7 and Conn. 112 two miles south of Falls Village; parking is available in a triangle north of Conn. 112. The southern end is on Conn. 4 0.9 mile west of Cornwall Bridge; vehicles can be parked 0.5 mile east where Conn. 4 and U.S. 7 intersect. Vehicular access also is possible along Sharon Mountain Road (mile 4.7/6.8) and West Cornwall Road (mile 6.7/4.8).

Maps—Refer to ATC's Map 3 for Massachusetts–Connecticut. For area detail, consult the USGS quadrangles listed at the top right of that map.

Shelters and campsites—No camping is permitted in this section, except at designated campsites or shelters. The only shelter in this section is Pine Swamp Brook Shelter (mile 5.6/5.9). Designated campsites are available at mile 0.4/11.1, 3.2/8.3, and 9.0/2.5. At mile 10.0/1.5, the Pine Knob Loop Trail leads 1.0 mile to Housatonic Meadows State Park campground.

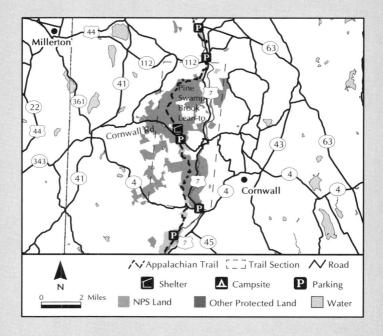

Millerton

Pine Swamp Brook Lean-to

Cornwall Rd.

Cornwall

↗⌁ Appalachian Trail ⌐ ¬ Trail Section ⋀ Road

N

0   2 Miles

◩ Shelter   ▲ Campsite   🅿 Parking

NPS Land   Other Protected Land   Water

SECTION HIGHLIGHTS

Northern end of section →

On U.S. 7 near intersection with Conn. 112. Parking available in triangle north of Conn. 112. Falls Village (ZIP Code 06031) is two miles north *via* U.S 7. West Cornwall is five miles south *via* U.S. 7.

Belter's Campsite →

Reached *via* blue-blazed trail from A.T. A privy is located at the campsite, and a spring is near A.T.

Hang Glider View →

One of the best views in this section is from here, with Bear Mountain and Mt. Everett in the distance. The view was first cut by hang-glider enthusiasts and looks north toward the Taconic Range. In the right foreground, part of the Lime Rock automobile race track is visible (and may be audible) from the Trail.

Sharon Mountain Campsite →

An open-sided "chum" privy is available. No water is at campsite—use brook 0.1 mile south on A.T. (may be dry in summer). No fires permitted.

Pine Swamp Brook Shelter →

Built in 1989, this shelter accommodates six, and several good tent sites are in the immediate vicinity. A privy is available. Water supply is nearby along a blue-blazed trail. Next shelter: south, 10.0 miles (Stewart Hollow Brook); north, 12.8 miles (Limestone Spring). This shelter (and this entire section of the Housatonic Highlands) is known among hikers for its fierce mosquitoes in warm months. The reason is glacially formed, upland, freshwater swamps, such as nearby Pine Swamp at the foot of Mt. Easter, which is more than one-half-mile wide and 600 feet above the river valley.

N-S	TRAIL DESCRIPTION	

0.0	**Northern end of section** is near junction of U.S. 7 and Conn. 112. Cross stile at northern end of section at west side of U.S. 7, below Sharon Mountain.	**11.5**
0.3	Reach Belter's Bump, scenic outlook named in honor of former owner Willis Belter.	**11.2**
0.4	Reach side trail to **Belter's Campsite**, below steep ridge-line climb to (or descent from) plateau of Sharon Mountain.	**11.1**
1.6	Pass viewpoints (both east and west) along ridge. The view west includes Kaaterskill High Peak in the Catskill Mountains of New York.	**9.9**
2.4	Pass scenic **Hang Glider View**.	**9.1**
3.2	Pass blue-blazed side trail to **Sharon Mountain Campsite**.	**8.3**
3.3	Cross brook, source of water for Sharon Mountain Campsite.	**8.2**
4.4	Skirt summit of Mt. Easter (1,350 feet).	**7.1**
4.7	Cross gravel Sharon Mountain Road, a state forest road.	**6.8**
5.6	Reach blue-blazed side trail to **Pine Swamp Brook Shelter**.	**5.9**
6.1	Just below a viewpoint, Trail passes between two huge boulders on path known as Roger's Ramp.	**5.4**

S-N

SECTION HIGHLIGHTS

West Cornwall Road →
Village of West Cornwall is three miles west, with supplies, restaurants, and stores. Sharon is four miles east with more facilities.

Caesar Road →
This old turnpike crossed the Housatonic on Young's Bridge in 1770.

Caesar Brook Campsite →
Water and an unenclosed "chum" privy are available.

Pine Knob Loop Trail →
Loops down to Housatonic Meadows State Park campground and back to A.T.

Housatonic Meadows State Park →
Campground along the Housatonic River offers campsites, toilet facilities, water, and other services. Fee charged.

Mohawk Trail →
This trail, once the route of the A.T., diverges here, crossing U.S. 7 at Cornwall Bridge as part of the Blue Trail system of the Connecticut Forest and Park Association. This "eastern route" was not called that when it was the A.T. The name came about during the controversy in the 1980s about relocating the Trail across the river (the "western route"). It rejoins the A.T. 24 miles north, near Falls Village. A loop of 37.2 miles is possible on the two trails (see pages 177–181 for route descriptions).

Southern end of section →
On Conn. 4, 0.9 mile west of Cornwall Bridge (ZIP Code 06754). Cars can be parked 0.5 mile east, where Conn. 4 joins U.S. 7 across from Cornwall Bridge. A general store, package store, post office, bank, and motel are available in town.

N-S   ┌─────── TRAIL DESCRIPTION ───────┐

6.7   Cross hard-surfaced **West Cornwall Road** in valley be-   **4.8**
tween two steep hills.

6.8   Cross Carse Brook on log bridge.   **4.7**

7.6   Cross abandoned Surdam Road.   **3.9**

9.0   Cross abandoned **Caesar Road**. Primitive **Caesar Brook**   **2.5**
Campsite is on knoll south of Caesar Brook.

9.4   Northern junction of **Pine Knob Loop Trail**, which leads   **2.1**
to a view and a 0.7-mile descent to **Housatonic Meadows**
State Park campground and U.S. 7.

9.8   Pine Knob, offers view of Housatonic Valley.   **1.7**

10.0   Pine Knob Loop Trail leads to U.S. 7 (1.0 mile) and **Hou-**   **1.5**
satonic Meadows State Park campground.

10.1   Cross Hatch Brook.   **1.4**

11.2   Side trail leads 0.1 mile to summit of Bread Loaf Mountain   **0.3**
and 0.7 mile to U.S. 7 Trailhead parking. This side trail
is an extension of the **Mohawk Trail**.

11.3   Cross dirt Old Sharon Road, which leads east toward   **0.2**
Cornwall Bridge.

11.4   Cross beautiful Guinea Brook on property of Walton   **0.1**
Fishing Club. Camping and fires are not permitted. During times of high water, hikers can avoid crossing the
brook by detouring on Old Sharon Road and Conn. 4.

11.5   **Southern end of section** on northern side of Conn. 4.   **0.0**

S-N

Conn. 4 to Conn. 341

11.1 MILES

Much of the Trail in this section is level, following an old road paralleling the Housatonic River through the townships of Sharon and Kent, in one of the most sustained "river-walks" on the entire A.T. This beautiful area, now owned by the National Park Service, had been the property of the Stanley Works of New Britain since the early twentieth century. Before a serious flood in 1936, the Trail crossed the river north of Kent, went through a culvert under railroad tracks, and climbed up Kent Falls to eventually reach Mohawk Mountain. Some of the original Trail is now part of the Connecticut Forest and Park Association's Blue Trail System. This section also bypasses an original loop through Macedonia Brook State Park. Most of the old Trail is now incorporated into the Macedonia Ridge Trail, maintained by a volunteer for the CFPA. Some of this section is on land formerly owned by the private Pond Mountain Trust, The Nature Conservancy (St. Johns Ledges), or the Kent School.

Road approaches—The northern end of this section is on Conn. 4, 0.9 mile west of Cornwall Bridge; vehicles can be parked 0.5 mile east where Conn. 4 and U.S. 7 intersect. At the southern end on Conn. 341, 0.8 mile west of kent and U.S. 7, daytime parking is possible 0.2 mile east at Schaghticoke Road. The Trail also crosses Dawn Hill Road (mile 1.5/9.6), a town road from Kent that terminates at North Kent Bridge (parking; mile 5.4/5.7), River Road (parking; mile 6.4/4.7), and Skiff Mountain Road (mile 8.3/2.8).

Maps—Refer to ATC's Map 4 for Massachusetts–Connecticut. For area detail, consult the USGS quadrangles listed at the top right of that map.

Shelters and Campsites—Camping is permitted only at Stewart Hollow Brook Shelter (mile 4.1/7.0) and campsites located near the shelter and at Silver Hill (mile 0.9/10.2). Campfires are not permitted.

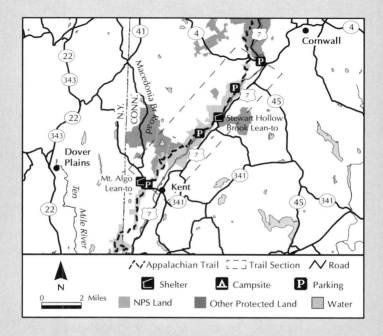

SECTION HIGHLIGHTS

Northern end of section →

On Conn. 4, 0.9 mile west of Cornwall Bridge (ZIP Code 06754). Cars can be parked 0.5 mile east, where Conn. 4 joins U.S. 7 across from Cornwall Bridge. A general store, package store, post office, bank, and motel are available in town.

Silver Hill Campsite →

Amenities here include an eating pavilion, water pump, and privy. There is no shelter. No fires permitted.

Swift's Bridge →

The last of three bridges at this site (named after an early settler) was destroyed by a flood in 1936. The Trail passes the largest big-tooth aspen tree in Connecticut, just south of the site of Swift's Bridge. Parking is available near the site of the former bridge. The road north along the river leads 1.5 miles to Cornwall Bridge.

Campsites →

Campsites are located south of Stony Brook. Group camping is north of brook. A privy is available. No fires permitted.

Stewart Hollow Brook Shelter →

Built in 1987 by AMC volunteers; accommodates six. Privy and camping sites nearby. No fires permitted. Water is located on the Trail south of the shelter. Next shelter: south, 7.3 miles (Mt. Algo); north, 10 miles (Pine Swamp Brook).

Pine plantation →

The Trail through a red-pine stand along the river was one of the most photographed sections of the A.T. Unfortunately, the red pines, which were planted in the early 1930s, suffered from a blight, and few have survived. Some of these pines were cut to supply logs for four of the shelters on the Connecticut A.T.

N-S

TRAIL DESCRIPTION

0.0   Northern **end of section** is on south side of Conn. 4, at the foot of steep, wooded Silver Hill.   **11.1**

0.1   Trail reaches lookout at height of land on northern side of Silver Hill.   **11.0**

0.9   Side trail (blue-blazed) to **Silver Hill Campsite**. A good view of the Housatonic Valley to the southeast.   **10.2**

1.5   Cross paved Dawn Hill Road.   **9.6**

1.7   ■ SOUTHBOUND hikers begin a five-mile river-walk. Cross dirt River Road, which parallels Housatonic River. A seasonal, untreated spring is a few feet north of Trail crossing. Following road south beyond the spring will lead to the site of **Swift's Bridge.** The Trail south of the old bridge follows a long-abandoned section of road below hayfields, locally known as Liner Farm. ■ NORTHBOUND hikers leave river and begin ascent onto ridge above the Housatonic Valley.   **9.4**

3.7   Cross Stony Brook. **Campsites** are nearby.   **7.4**

4.1   Cross Stewart Hollow Brook—may be dry. **Stewart Hollow Brook Shelter** and campsite are nearby. The Trail south of the shelter passes through a **pine plantation**.   **7.0**

S-N

North Kent Bridge →

The A.T. formerly crossed the river at this bridge, before a 1936 flood wiped it out. Cars may be parked here. Just north of the bridge gate, the "red house" site is kept open by the Connecticut AMC Trails Committee as a reminder of the days when as many as 17 children were ferried across the river daily to attend school in Kent village.

River Road →

Conn. 341 is three miles south of the Trail's intersection with River Road at base of St. Johns Ledges. Parking available. A group of houses here was known as "Alder City."

St. Johns Ledges →

These rock cliffs, named after an eighteenth-century owner, Timothy St. Johns, are used frequently for rock-climbing instruction.

N-S

| TRAIL DESCRIPTION |

5.4 Terminus of town road running north along the river from Kent. Pass site of **North Kent Bridge** (or Flanders Bridge). From this point to the Sharon township line (south of Swift's Bridge), the road has been legally abandoned and is closed to vehicles. *Hikers should keep close to river on road trail, avoiding all woods roads to west.* **5.7**

5.8 Cross mountain brook. **5.3**

6.4 Trail intersects with **River Road** at base of St. Johns Ledges. ■ SOUTHBOUND hikers begin climb to St. Johns Ledges. ■ NORTHBOUND hikers begin five-mile river-walk. **4.7**

6.9 Trail crosses top of **St. Johns Ledges**. North of the overlook, the ledges are traversed by means of 90 rock steps installed by an AMC Trail crew from the White Mountains, replacing an eroded old trail. The view overlooks the Housatonic Valley and the town of Kent. **4.2**

St. Johns Ledges

S-N

Skiff Mountain Road →

Leads southeast to the town of Kent.

Kent →

Founded in 1739, Kent was one of seven townships comprising Connecticut's "western lands." In 1694, the Rev. Benjamin Wadsworth referred to Kent, now the hub of an area of fine estates, as a "hideous, howling wilderness." The approximately 11,000 acres between the Housatonic and the New York border, which include the Trail, were originally set aside by the General Assembly for use by native Americans but were annexed to Kent a few years later. Despite prohibitions by the assembly, Indian lands were leased or sold, and, by 1752, only 18 Indian families remained out of the approximately 100 from several weakened original tribes who had lived there a few years earlier.

Numeral Rock Trail →

Numeral Rock overlooks town of Kent. The blue-blazed trail here is the former route of the A.T., intersecting with Conn. 341 0.2 mile east of the A.T. It serves as a bypass route when Macedonia Brook floods.

Southern end of section →

On Conn. 341, 0.8 mile west of Kent (ZIP Code 06757). There is no parking at the Trailhead. The town offers groceries, restaurants, and most services, including a backpacking store. Strobles Bakery and Cookery on Main Street is a particular favorite of hikers, residents, and weekenders alike. Cars can be parked during the day 0.2 mile east, at the junction of Conn. 341 and Schaghticoke Road, but overnight parking is not recommended.

N-S

| | TRAIL DESCRIPTION | |

7.6	Reach Caleb's Peak (1,160 feet). Ledge outcrop has fine views of Housatonic River to southeast. Trail traverses steep section nearest top.	**3.5**
8.1	Viewpoint at ledge outcropping.	**3.0**
8.3	Cross **Skiff Mountain Road**.	**2.8**
8.4	Cross Choggam Brook, usually dry in late summer.	**2.7**
10.3	Ledge provides view of **Kent** and Housatonic Valley.	**0.8**
10.5	Junction with blue-blazed trail leading to **Numeral Rock.**	**0.6**
11.0	Macedonia Brook. Cross on log bridge. ■ SOUTHBOUND hikers then cross a pasture south of the brook. ■ NORTHBOUNDers begin a steep ascent.	**0.1**
11.1	**Southern end of section** on the northern side of Conn. 341.	**0.0**

S-N

Conn. 341 to Hoyt Road (N.Y.)

11.5 MILES

The A.T. in this section crosses the ridge of Schaghticoke and Algo mountains, providing many views of the valley. The Trail follows the Housatonic River gorge south of Bull's Bridge and crosses the Ten Mile River on the 120-foot Ned Anderson Memorial Bridge, built in 1983. This section of the Housatonic, called the "Great Bend," is very scenic. On the ridge of Schaghticoke Mountain, the A.T. very briefly passes through the Schaghticoke Tribal Nation reservation. After negotiating Ten Mile Hill, the Connecticut section southbound ends at the New York state line at Hoyt Road.

Road approaches—The northern end is on Conn. 341, 0.8 mile west of Kent and U.S. 7; daytime parking is possible 0.2 mile east at Schaghticoke Road. The southern end is on Hoyt Road just west of the Connecticut–New York line and can be reached by way of N.Y. 55, 0.25 mile to the north and 3.3 miles east of Webatuck and Wingdale. Up to three cars may be parked at the Trailhead. The Trail intersects Schaghticoke Road at mile 7.1/4.4; it intersects with Bulls Bridge Road at mile 7.4/4.1 (parking available near the bridge). Conn. 55 crosses the Trail at mile 10.8/0.7.

Maps—Refer to ATC's Map 4 for Massachusetts–Connecticut. For area detail, consult the USGS quadrangles listed at the top right of that map. This map extends almost 20 Trail miles into New York, favoring hikes to and from the Metro–North train station on N.Y. 22 and other adventures hiking to or from Connecticut.

Shelters and campsites—This section has two shelters, Mt. Algo Shelter (mile 0.;3/11.2) and Ten Mile River Shelter (mile 8.7/2.8). Designated camping is available at the confluence of the Housatonic and Ten Mile rivers (mile 8.5/3.0) and at Schaghticoke Mountain Campsite (mile 3.2/8.3). No campfires are permitted at any of those sites.

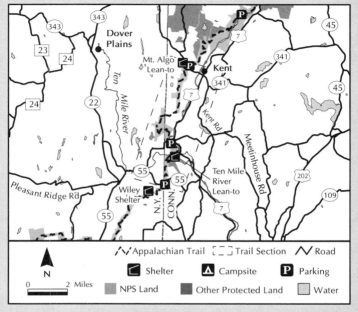

In these states, "shelter" and "lean-to" are synonymous.

SECTION HIGHLIGHTS

Northern end of section →

On Conn. 341, 0.8 mile west of Kent (ZIP Code 06757). The town offers groceries, restaurants, and most services, including a back-packing store; bus service is available. Cars can be parked during the day 0.2 mile east, at the junction of Conn. 341 and Schaghticoke Road, but overnight parking is not recommended.

Mt. Algo Shelter →

Built in 1986; accommodates six. Camping nearshelter. A privy is nearby. Water is available on the blue-blazed trail from the A.T. No fires are permitted. Next shelter: south, 8.4 miles (Ten Mile river); north, 7.3 miles (Stewart Hollow Brook).

Schaghticoke Mountain Campsite →

Campsite with privy. Water available nearby. No fires permitted.

Schaghticoke Tribal Nation Reservation →

The Trail crosses this state-recognized reservation on a narrow corridor of land that for more than a decade has been the subject of litigation connected with the tribe's pursuit of federal recognition and of more land just north of the Trail (which NPS seeks to buy from the Preston Mountain Club). The reservation, home of the Schaghticoke Tribal Nation, is the only native American land through which the A.T. passes. Its settled area consists of a handful of dwellings near the river. The original area of the tribes, the remnants of which comprise the Schaghticokes, was much larger, extending to and including the confluence of the Housatonic and Ten Mile rivers. This river corridor is one of the most important areas of native and Euroamerican heritage in northwestern Connecticut and was the area's last major native American stronghold. Remnants of encampments nearby date to more than 4,000 years ago. The valley of the Ten Mile was the natural highway to the Housatonic Valley. Early historical accounts mention that the floodplain was covered with Indian cornfields and wigwams. The Kent corridor has an extremely high archaeological sensitivity. Many undiscovered prehistoric and historic sites can be expected beneath the area's soil.

N-S	TRAIL DESCRIPTION	
0.0	**Northern end of section** on south side of Conn. 341 at foot of Mt. Algo.	11.5
0.1	Cross woods road in hemlock woods.	**11.4**
0.3	Blue-blazed side trail leads 200 feet to water and **Mt. Algo Shelter**.	**11.2**
0.9	Cross height of land on Mt. Algo.	**10.6**
1.3	Cross Thayer Brook. The path south of the brook is rocky.	**10.2**
1.8	Reach high point (1,403 feet) on northeast side of Schaghticoke Mountain massif. Good views to south from ledges.	**9.7**
2.4	Pass viewpoint. Winter views are plentiful along this ridge.	**9.1**
3.2	Trail crosses brook just above Rattlesnake Den, a ravine with large hemlocks and jumbled boulders. Reliable water source here, except in very dry years. Pass side trail to **Schaghticoke Mountain Campsite**.	**8.3**
3.5	Trail enters Dry Gulch, another rocky ravine with steep approaches from either direction.	**8.0**
3.8	Reach Indian Rocks, an outlook to the east near **Schaghticoke Tribal Nation reservation.** Traverse eastern side of Schaghticoke Mountain, with winter views of Housatonic Valley and U.S. 7 below.	**7.7**

SECTION HIGHLIGHTS

Schaghticoke Road→

Leads north along the Housatonic River, through the Indian reservation and past Kent School, to the town of Kent.

Bulls Bridge →

One of two remaining covered bridges in Connecticut that still permit traffic. The bridge, a short distance east of a parking area on Bulls Bridge Road, was named after an early settler who had an inn near the present location of the Bulls Bridge Inn that often catered to George Washington, among others. Washington's horse is said to have fallen off or through the bridge here. Across the road from the parking lot is a dam built in 1902—worth a visit when the water is high. Just below the gorge on the other side of the river are the remains of an old blast furnace. Kent was second to Salisbury in the eighteenth century as a source of high-quality iron ore.

Bulls Bridge Road→

In New York becomes Dogtail Corners Road, once a direct route between Hartford and Poughkeepsie, New York. Now leads west, by way of Dogtail Corners, to the New York communities of Webatuck and Wingdale, and east, by way of Bulls Bridge (0.5 mile), to U.S. 7 and the Connecticut community of South Kent. Parking is available near the covered bridge.

N-S

TRAIL DESCRIPTION

4.2 Marker at Connecticut–New York border, one of three crossings in this section. Between here and Schaghticoke Road, Southbound hikers begin descent along numerous switchbacks, crossing the Connecticut–New York border again (no marker).   **7.3**

7.1 Trail intersects west side of hard-surfaced **Schaghticoke Road** in Connecticut, at foot of Schaghticoke Mountain. ■ Northbound hikers begin ascent along numerous switchbacks to Connecticut–New York border (no marker) before reaching height of land. ■ Southbound hikers begin road-walk toward **Bulls Bridge**.   **4.4**

7.4 Schaghticoke Road intersects **Bulls Bridge Road**. ■ Southbound hikers cross road and ascend a rise. ■ Northbound follow Schaghticoke Road north.   **4.1**

7.9 Trail turns 90 degrees at intersection with old farm road. ■ Southbound hikers turn right along west bank of Housatonic River on old farm road and then a scenic riverside trail. ■ Northbound hikers turn left before reaching Bulls Bridge Road and ascend.   **3.6**

8.4 Pass through gap in stone wall. ■ Northbound hikers follow scenic riverbank trail toward Bulls Bridge. ■ Southbound hikers pass under powerlines, with view of Ten Mile Hill to south.   **3.1**

8.4 Cross small brook.   **3.1**

S-N

Ned Anderson Memorial Bridge →

The Trail crosses Ten Mile River on the Ned Anderson Memorial Bridge, built in 1983. The steel-reinforced span was prefabricated, shipped by a truck, and installed with a crane. Ned Anderson was a locally beloved "Renaissance man" from Sherman who designed, built, and, for 20 years, maintained the original Trail in Connecticut while running a 165-acre farm. It was then a project of his "Housatonic Trail Club" (1929-1949), later incorporated into the Connecticut Forest and Park Association.

Ten Mile River Camping Area →

A camping area is in the field south of the bridge, as is a water pump and privy. No fires allowed.

Ten Mile River Shelter →

Built in 1996, this shelter accommodates six. Privy nearby. Water pump is near shelter. No campfires permitted.

Herrick Trail →

Leads around Ten Mile Hill, one mile, to view of Housatonic River.

Conn. 55 →

Leads west four miles to the New York communities of Webatuck and Wingdale and east to the Housatonic River and U.S. 7. No parking at road crossing, but a large parking lot is on the south side of Conn. 55 near the Connecticut–New York state line and close to the Trail.

Southern end of section →

Reached by way of N.Y. 55, which is 0.25 mile north of the Trailhead and 3.3 miles east of the communities of Webatuck and Wingdale. Restaurants, lodging, groceries, and a hardware store are available. One mile beyond Wingdale is a station of the Metro–North commuter train line from New York City. Up to three cars may be parked at Hoyt Road. The Wiley Shelter is located 1.2 miles south of the end of the section on the A.T. in New York (see *Appalachian Trail Guide to New York–New Jersey* and/or Map 4 with this guide.)

TRAIL DESCRIPTION

Bulls Bridge

8.5 Cross Ten Mile River on **Ned Anderson Memorial Bridge**. **3.0**
Pass **Ten Mile River Camping Area** in field south of bridge.

8.7 Blue-blazed side trail to **Ten Mile River Shelter**. **2.8**

9.0 Cross dirt road. **2.5**

9.2 Intermittent spring. **2.3**

9.3 Trail turns sharply at both ends of gradual elevation **2.2**
change along old woods road.

9.6 Junction with blue-blazed **Herrick Trail** to east. **1.9**

9.7 Reach top of Ten Mile Hill (1,000 feet). Views of the **1.8**
Housatonic Valley can be had along a short, unmarked
side trail. Start gradual descent immediately.

10.8 Cross **Conn. 55**. **0.7**

11.4 Top of ridge. **0.1**

11.5 Cross Connecticut–New York state line on northern side **0.0**
of Hoyt Road, the **southern end of section**.

Major Side Trails

A significant characteristic of the Appalachian Trail in both Massachusetts and Connecticut is its place as the trunk of an extensive system of shorter trails that not only allow loop hikes but also exploration of other terrain throughout the western mountains of these two states. The descriptions that follow are basic; further details can be found in such AMC books as *Best Day Hikes in the Berkshires* and *Best Day Hikes in Connecticut,* both of which can be ordered on line at <www.outdoors.org>.

Northern Berkshires Trails

The significant side trails to the Appalachian Trail in Massachusetts are in either the Mt. Greylock area or south of Jug End.

The most scenic and popular section of the A.T. in Massachusetts (with the possible exception of Mt. Greylock) is from Jug End south to the Connecticut line. The northernmost part of the Connecticut A.T. is also the most popular in that state. The two sections can be treated as one, extending from Jug End Road in South Egremont, Massachusetts, to Conn. 41 in Salisbury, Connecticut, a distance of 16.7 Trail miles or 11 road miles, accessible from three side trails.

The 1.5-mile-long **Elbow Trai**l starts at the Berkshire School campus on Mass. 41 and reaches the A.T. 1.5 miles north of Mt. Everett and 2.8 miles south of Jug End Road. It is maintained by Berkshire School.

Race Brook Falls Trail goes from a parking area on Mass. 41, three miles south of Jug End Road, across state land to the A.T. 0.7 mile south of Mt. Everett. The trail is roughly two miles long, with three brook crossings and side trails to falls. A designated campsite above the last falls is within 0.5 mile of the A.T. junction.

Undermountain Trail starts in Connecticut on Conn. 41, 7.3 miles from Jug End Road and 3.5 miles north of Salisbury. It is 1.9 miles long and connects to the A.T. one mile south of Bear Mountain. The most-used access trail in Connecticut, it is maintained by the Connecticut Chapter of the Appalachian Mountain Club.

For many years, the Mt. Greylock State Reservation has had an extensive trail system. While not all of those are side trails to the Appalachian Trail, some are described here because of their proximity to the A.T. and their interest to hikers. Shelters are available on some trails, with a large campground on Sperry Road. Since 1983, many of these trails have been maintained by AMC Adopt-a-Trail volunteers in cooperation with the Massachusetts Department of Conservation and Recreation's Division of Forests and Parks.

MASSACHUSETTS SECTION ONE

Broad Brook Trail from White Oaks Road
Williamstown, Massachusetts — Pownal, Vermont
4.1 miles
Maintained by the Williams College Outing Club

Trail Description, South to North

0.0   Parking lot beside Broad Brook and North Adams watershed service road on east side of White Oaks Road.

0.8   Trail narrows, and footpath is in poor condition when going over large hummocks and irregular terrain.

1.1   Trail crosses Broad Brook, which does not have a bridge or stepping stones; hard to cross even at low water during summer months.

1.5   Junction with Agawon Trail on northwest side of Broad Brook, immediately after which Broad Brook Trail crosses brook in an upstream, diagonal manner, making use of rocky islands in stream.

1.6   Trail leaves brook, ascending a steep ridge to east.

1.7   After slabbing side of steep ridge, trail descends shortly to brook.

2.2   After crossing brook again, trail follows new logging road for short distance before logging road ascends hillside; trail stays on northwest side of brook.

2.5   Trail crosses northwest branch of Broad Brook and ascends a steep esker between two branches of brook.

3.1   After traveling along floodplain, trail crosses a northeast branch of Broad Brook at unusual cliff and boulder pool.

3.3   Trail soon crosses large tributary and rises steeply through a precipitous hemlock slope to plateau of hardwoods.

3.5   Trail drops steeply and crosses another tributary.

3.8   After following northeast side of tributary, trail hits unpaved road; 150 feet to west is junction of old grassy road that follows brook north to County Road.

4.1   Trail turns east along unpaved road, and blue blazes end where A.T. crosses unpaved road on way to Seth Warner Shelter (0.4 mile).

Pine Cobble Trail to North Hoosic Road, Williamstown, Massachusetts
2.3 miles
Maintained by the Williams college Outing Club

Trail Description, North to South

0.0   Junction of A.T. and Pine Cobble Trail. Leaving A.T. on top of East Mountain, trail goes overjagged marble cobbles, descending into stand of white birch.

0.5   Trail meets short trail to Pine Cobble overlook of North Adams and Williamstown. Main trail turns right and steeply downhill.

0.9   Rock seat beside old burn.

1.0   Junction of old Pine Cobble Trail that went down cliffslide to Bear Springs; new trail curves to west to avoid cliff.

1.3   Pine Cobble Trail joins old trail at bottom of cliff, also the junction with the lower end of the Class of '98 Trail.

1.4   Trail turns off old road to south, left, and gradually steepens down narrow ridge on east side of college housing development.

1.8   Trail turns west on small plateau and slabs southern hillside.

2.1   After following along rim of road bank, trail crosses road to parking lot for A.T.

2.3   For local hikers, trail continues and parallels development road until Pine Cobble Trail ends at North Hoosic Road

Class of '98 Trail to Pine Cobble Trail
2.0 miles
Maintained by the Williams College Outing Club

Trail serves as an alternative access to the A.T./L.T. or provides a loop option using the Pine Cobble Trail and A.T.

Trail Description, North to South

0.0   Trail leaves A.T. to west and begins lengthy sidehill descent, skirting west side of mountain, eventually travelling in a southerly direction.

1.1   Trail turns sharply west and skirts a boulder-filled drainage.

1.2   Trail turns sharply south and enters boulder field, descending steeply. Hikers should use caution.

1.3   After one more switchback, terrain flattens, and trail enters sapling grove.

1.4   Trail is on old woods road.

1.5   Chestnut Trail intersects from west; it continues 1.5 miles to Chestnut Street.

1.8   Woods road turns west; Class of '98 Trail continues south over boulders

2.1   Junction with Pine Cobble Trail, 0.8 mile from parking area.

MASSACHUSETTS SECTION TWO

Bellows Pipe Trail
3.7 miles

Trail Description, North to South

0.0   Bernard's Farm, at 90-degree corner, last farm on Notch Road.

0.3   Trail follows old North Adams watershed access road, staying on more westerly fork.

0.7   Sixteen brooks, half of which are dry in fall, cross trail as it leaves more level reservoir area and starts uphill.

1.4   Trail enters Mt. Greylock State Reservation where line of blue-blazed trees crosses perpendicular to trail.

2.0   After steady uphill climb, trail leaves Mt. Greylock State Reservation. Blue blazes parallel the trail for a short distance as trail enters a flatter, overgrown, field-type terrain.

2.1   Steep drop into dry ravine and climb on south side, into open and abandoned apple orchard.

2.2   Trail reenters Mt. Greylock State Reservation and goes through thick red-spruce and red-pine grove in saddle between Ragged Mountain and Mt. Greylock. Named Bellows Pipe after a wind effect here.

2.3   Trail to Ragged Mountain heads east in same area that old Bellows Pipe Ski Trail used to come down off Mt. Greylock and heads toward Thunderbolt Ski Trail and Adams, Massachusetts.

2.5   Orange-paint blazing on trees designates 0.8-mile radius from war memorial on summit of Mt. Greylock as a "no hunting" area.

2.6   Immediately after crossing a deep ravine, trail takes a sharp angle turn to northwest at a junction with old access road to Thunderbolt Trail.

2.7   Trail passes just to west of three-sided lean-to (camping permitted) with wooden floor,

2.8   Trail joins old Bellows Pipe Ski Trail. Crosses orange-blazed "no-hunting" zone again as it heads toward ridge.

3.2   Junction of snowmobile trail (old road) south to Thunderbolt Trail, where Bellows Pipe Trail turns steeply northwest in a long series of switchbacks.

3.4   At fourth switchback, trail turns northwest again while old road leads south to Thunderbolt Trail.

3.7   After several more switchbacks, Bellows Pipe Trail reaches junction with A.T.

Cheshire Harbor Trail
2.6 miles

Trail Description, East to West

0.0   End of West Mountain Road (Old Shultz Farm).

0.1   After 100 yards, old farm road ends.

0.5   Trail goes around first hairpin turn, after which Mt. Greylock State Reservation boundary diagonally crosses "Old Adams Road" to right.

0.6 At second hairpin turn, a side trail goes off to southeast.

0.8 At third hairpin turn, Peck's Brook can be heard in ravine below.

1.0 After passing fourth hairpin turn, trail and "Old Adams Road" divide at fifth hairpin turn, with Cheshire Harbor Trail heading northwest.

1.5 Follow some badly eroded sections as trail steepens.

1.7 Side trail (Peck's Brook Connector) goes steeply down into ravine to northeast and steeply up to Gould Trail.

1.8 Trail bends sharply to north and levels off for a while.

2.3 Trail enters gentle S-turn and then continues straight north before crossing Peck's Brook.

2.6 Cheshire Harbor Trail ends at junctionof A.T. and Rockwell Road.

Deer Hill Loop Trail
1.7 miles (in Mt. Greylock State Reservation)

0.0 Junction of Deer Hill Trail and Hopper Trail between Sperry and Rockwell roads on old carriage road.

0.1 Spring house that feeds campground and old CCC dam can be seen downhill from trail.

0.4 Old carriage road, used as Deer Hill Trail, heads southwest and crosses Sperry Road.

0.8 Trail takes a sharp downhill turn to west and follows a deep ravine, while ski trail continues straight across bridge toward Rockwell Road.

1.2 Entering stand of old hemlocks, trail descends sharply past a lean-to.

1.4 Down into roaring brook, trail crosses between pools and ascends steeply up north side of ravine for 200 feet before making a turn to parallel gorge.

1.5 First of many rock steps as trail nears falls area of Roaring Brook.

1.7 Trail heads out of dark, moist, evergreen ravine and into flatter hardwood forest to junction with Roaring Brook Trail and end.

Gould Trail to Peck's Brook Lean-to
1 mile (in Mt. Greylock State Reservation)

Trail Description, West to East

0.0   Start at trailhead where Rockwell Road intersects Notch Road.

0.5   Trail descends past two small brooks.

0.8   Descending along gently sloping ridge, trail returns to parallel small brook for short distance.

0.9   Immediately after crossing orange-blazed, ¾-mile "no-hunting" boundary of Greylock summit, side trail to shelter heads south from Gould Farm Trail and crosses small brook. Main trail continues 1 mile to West Mountain Road in Adams.

1.0   Trail dead-ends at Peck's Brook Lean-to with Peck's Brook Falls another 150 feet to south.

Trail to Robinson Point Vista
0.3 mile

Trail Description, East to West

0.0   Trail leaves road just downhill from parking space (two cars) on Notch Road (yellow sign painted on road).

0.2   After steep downhill path, trail crosses swamp and brook.

0.3   Trail ends at spectacular view of inner Hopper Ravines, Mt. Prospect, and old Mt. Hope Farm in Williamstown.

Hopper Trail
3.4 miles

Trail Description, West to East

Note: At end of Hopper Road (off Mass. 43) in Williamstown, parking is available at designated parking lot beside information kiosk near the Haley Farm.

0.0   Farm gate on road leading between two pastures.

0.1   Reach second gate on level farm road; stone walls on both sides.

0.3   Junction of Money Brook Trail (farm road leading downhill to brook), with Hopper Trail leading into overgrown pasture on right.

0.5   After taking right fork on Hopper Trail through pasture, trail enters woods.

1.4   Side trail downhill to Money Brook Trail goes off Hopper Trail to left.

1.5   Springs emerge from hillside and run across trail to provide only water on trail.

2.3   After a steady climb, quite steep at times, trail levels off in red-spruce grove and comes out at Site 16 in Sperry Road camping area.

2.4   Hopper Trail follows Sperry Road for 0.1 mile and, opposite campground contact station, turns left into woods on steep, wet trail.

2.5   Remains of old CCC log dam and spring house can be seen below small cliff and waterfall on right.

2.6   Hopper Trail turns sharply left as Deer Hill Trail (Old Greylock Stage Coach Road) enters from right.

3.1   Follow old road up Mt. Greylock. Overlook Trail comes in on left.

3.2   Hopper Trail meets Rockwell Road at hairpin turn. To find A.T., walk up paved road 100 yards to next hairpin curve; A.T. emerges from woods (heading south).

3.4   After short distance back into woods, Hopper Trail ends at junction with A.T.

3.5   A divided Hopper Trail allows hikers to bypass Rockwell Road and arrive on the A.T.

Overlook Trail to Hopper Trail (Loop Trail)
1.6 miles

0.0   Junction of Overlook Trail and A.T., south from Mt. Greylock, near TV station.

0.4   After following graded old carriage road, trail crosses Notch Road.

1.0   Third overlook sign indicates side trail to view of Hopper Valley and Stony Ledge.

1.4   Another overlook with view of Campground Ridge and Stony Ledge.

1.5   Trail crosses ravine and stream from a summit pond.

1.6   Trail ends at junction with Hopper Trail, 100 yards from S curve on Rockwell Road.

Money Brook Trail
3.5 miles

Note: At end of Hopper Road (off Mass. 43) in Williamstown, parking is available at designated parking lot at Haley Farm.

Trail Description, South to North

0.0   Farm gate on road leading between two pastures.

0.1   Reach second gate on level farm road, with stone walls on both sides.

0.3   Junction of Hopper Trail (on right through overgrown pasture) with Money Brook Trail, which follows farm road downhill.

0.5   Brookside pasture; trail goes through last fence.

0.7   Trail comes to crossing of Hopper Brook and continues on old logging road.

1.2   At junction of two main tributaries that form Hopper Brook is a large pool, immediately after which trail takes sharp right across Money Brook tributary. Short-cut to Hopper Trail goes off to right as Money Brook Trail continues upstream.

1.6   Cross tributary to Money Brook just before trail crosses main Money Brook again. Crossing can be difficult during times of high water.

1.7   Mt. Prospect Trail goes steeply up from brook to left as Money Brook Trail goes up onto shelf parallel to brook.

2.5   Trail crosses Money Brook for last time and ascends steeply with switchbacks through hemlock grove.

2.8   Hairpin turn on trail; side trail to Money Brook falls off to right on corner.

3.0   After steep sidehill ascent, trail levels off in beech and northern hardwood forest, where a short-cut trail to Notch Road and A.T. comes in on right.

3.3   Money Brook Trail stays level as it passes through thick red-spruce grove where Wilbur Clearing Lean-to. A.T. is on left.

3.5   Money Brook Trail goes by a spring and continues through thick red-spruce grove, ending at junction with A.T.

Connecticut Side Trails

All blue-blazed side trails referenced in the Trail descriptions are listed here, north to south, for convenience.

Paradise Lane Trail is 2.1 miles long. It starts 0.7 mile south of Sages Ravine Brook crossing and meets the Undermountain Trail 1.1 miles west of Conn. 41.

Undermountain Trail is 1.9 miles long. It starts on the A.T. 2.3 miles from Sages Ravine Brook crossing and meets Undermountain Road (Conn. 41) 3.5 miles north of Salisbury.

Lions Head Bypass Trail is only 0.1 mile long. It is a bad-weather detour of Lions Head.

Lions Head Trail is the former route of the A.T. and leads 0.4 mile from the present A.T. to the end of Bunker Hill Road.

Limestone Spring Trail is 1.3 miles long. It starts on the A.T. 3.2 miles from U.S. 44 and goes to the Limestone Spring Lean-to, then continues 0.7 mile to Sugar Hill Road.

Pine Knob Loop Trail coincides with the A.T. for 0.3 mile, and leads 0.7 mile to U.S. 7 near Housatonic Meadows, one mile north of Conn. 4.

Breadloaf Mountain Trail, part of the Mohawk Trail, is 0.8 mile long, starts from U.S. 7 at Cornwall Bridge and intersects the A.T.

Numeral Rock Trail is the old A.T., 0.6 mile, for use when the pasture on Conn. 341 is flooded by Macedonia Brook.

MOHAWK–APPALACHIAN LOOP TRAIL

(Excerpted from the 17th edition of the *Connecticut Walk Book,* with permission from the Connecticut Forest and Park Association.)

The 24-mile Mohawk Trail, the old A.T., is now part of the 825-mile Blue Trail System of the Connecticut Forest and Park Association. It can also be considered a side trail to the A.T. as both ends intersect the present A.T., at Falls Village and Cornwall Bridge. A suggested four-day backpacking trip uses this loop in a counter-clockwise direction:

Day 1	Cornwall Bridge to YCC Lean-to	9.1 miles
Day 2	YCC Lean-to to Pine Knoll Lean-to	11.0 miles
Day 3	Pine Knoll Lean-to to Pine Swamp Brook Shelter	10.7 miles
Day 4	Pine Swamp Brook Shelter to Cornwall Bridge	6.4 miles

Total: 37.2 miles

The Mohawk Trail was established as a blue-blazed hiking trail on May 8, 1988. It follows the traditional route of the Appalachian Trail, which was not needed after a new route was opened through Sharon from Conn. 4 to Falls Village.

Two events since the opening had a significant negative impact on the old Trail route. The first was the closing of the trail between Echo Rock and Valley Road in the fall of 1988. Then, damage to the Cathedral Pines area by a tornado on July 10, 1989, effectively closed the trail there. During 1992, work was completed on relocations through both those areas.

The northbound Mohawk Trail starts at the Appalachian Trail, at a point 0.3 mile north of its crossing of Conn. 4, 0.5 mile west of Cornwall Bridge. A complete trail description follows.

Appalachian Trail to Cornwall Bridge
0.00   Go northeast on blue-blazed trail.
0.10   Reach summit of Breadloaf Mountain (1,050 feet); excellent view southeast.
0.15   Begin steep descent *via* switchbacks.
0.25   Pass through opening in large stone wall.
0.60   Reach U.S. 7 at parking area.
0.70   Cross Housatonic River on concrete bridge.
0.90   Reach grassy triangle in village of Cornwall Bridge, at junction of Conn. 4 and U.S. 7 (parking on Conn. 4).

Cornwall Bridge to Essex Hill Road
0.0   From eastside of triangle at the intersection of Conn. 4 and U.S. 7 (parking on Conn. 4), follow Dark Entry Road.
0.9   Cross Bonny Brook, and then pass dam.

1.5   Cross brook again. *Please stay on the trail.*

2.5   Reach Echo Rock (1,450 feet) on side of Coltsfoot Mountain. Spectacular view of Cornwall Valley with Mohawk Mountain in the distance. Continue north, descending gradually.

3.1   View to northwest over grove of white birch. Continue north, ascending gradually.

3.6   Reach grassy, open summit (1,250 feet). Continue north through logged area.

4.0   Reach summit of northern ridge of Coltsfoot Mountain (1,150 feet); restricted views east and west of Cornwall Valley. Contiue north along ridgecrest through evidence of heavy tornado damage.

4.1   Short (50 feet) side trail on left to view north.

4.4   Turn east and then south, descending rapidly, slabbing steep eastern slope of ridge. *Use extreme caution,* especially under slippery conditions.

4.5   View of Coltsfoot Valley.

4.8   Near base of eastern slope, turn north, and sidehill the ridge through increasingly severe tornado devastation.

5.4   Cross Furnace Brook on telephone-pole bridge built by Connecticut AMC volunteers in 1992. Then, bear northwest through boggy area and fields.

5.5   Follow electric fence to a lawn; cross the lawn.

5.6   Reach Jewel Street in Cornwall village. Go east on Jewel Street past Marvelwood School.

5.8   Turn right onto Valley Road.

6.2   Turn left into Essex Hill Road, and continue to parking lot on northern side.

Essex Hill Road to Bunker Hill

0.00   From large boulder in parking lot on north side of Essex Hill Road, go east through brush and briars; then climb steeply up side of hill through grove of large hemlocks.

0.16   Reach top of hill; descend into swale.

0.20   Climb again, with switchbacks, through blowdowns and slash. This area, known as Cathedral Pines, was one of the most beautiful stands of evergreens in the state. It was devastated by a tornado in July 1989. The Nature Conservancy, which owns this land, is conducting a study of the tornado damage. Take time to notice nature's work of destruction and regeneration.

0.32   Join old woods road.

0.36   Cross stone wall.

0.45   Turn left on Essex Hill Road.

0.52   Turn right on Great Hollow Road; follow it to a driveway to private home on left.

0.68   Follow private driveway to gate; cross bridge over brook; then climb hill on logging road through area of blowdowns and sash.

0.95   Turn left from logging road onto Trail; recross logging road; then climb right bank-views to the west.

1.07   Leave cut-over area, and descend to brook.

1.12   Cross large brook.

1.15   Cross seasonal brook.

1.19   Reach edge of ski trail.

1.20   Reach stone wall. A short bushwhack to left through briars to ski trail provides views north and west.

1.25   Reach left bank of brook; turn left.

1.27   Cross stone wall.

1.28   Cross stone wall; turn right.

1.30   Cross stone wall.

1.39   Join old ski trail; turn right.

1.45   Reach junction with Mattatuck Trail on right. This is the northern terminus of the Mattatuck. The summit of Mohawk Mountain is 1.4 miles southeast on the Mattatuck Trail. Turn left.

1.50   Pass small stone tower, the upper terminus of the Mohawk Mountain ski lift. Good views west and north to Bear Mountain and Mt. Everett.

1.70   Cross Tourney Road Camping Zone. YCC (Youth Conservation Corps) Lean-to is just beyond.

2.90   Reach Camping Zone Lean-to.

3.00   Reach Conn. 4 at top of Bunker Hill.

Bunker Hill to Dean's Ravine

0.0   Cross to north side of Conn. 4.

0.1   Turn left, and ascend Red Mountain (1,653 feet). Red Mountain Lean-to (Camping Zone) is straight ahead 0.14 mile from Conn. 4.

0.3   After trail begins to level out, turn right at rock outcrop.

0.4   Open view to northwest. Turn right.

0.7   Open ledge with views to east. Turn left, and descend through laurel.

1.0   Turn left.

1.4   Turn right.

1.6   Turn right on Johnson Road, and continue on Indian Lane. No blue blazes on Johnson Road.

2.5   Cross Conn. 43, and continue on Trail.

4.2   Cross Lake Road.

5.8   Cross dirt Ford Hill Road (no parking).

7.5   Pass wildlife pond. Then, in the next 1.5 miles, the trail crosses three state forest roads.

9.7   Follow Wickwire Road to Pine Knoll Lean-to (unreliable spring).

10.8   Reach Music Mountain Road and Dean's Ravine picnic area (parking).

Dean's Ravine to Falls Village

0.0   From Dean's Ravine picnic area (parking), follow brook steeply downstream to bottom of ravine and former A.T. camping area.

0.6   Turn left from brook and then right on Music Mountain Road.

0.7   Turn right, and climb embankment into woods, ascending steeply over rocky surface.

2.0   Reach open ledges of "Lookout Point," with view west over the Housatonic River Valley

2.3   After more steep climbing, reach summit of Barrack Mountain on North Rock (1,230 feet). Excellent views.

2.6   After steep and rocky descent, cross U.S. 7, and enter grounds of Housatonic Valley Regional High School. Join the cross-country course briefly, and pass the VoAg Christmas-tree stand (parking).

2.7   Cross railroad tracks to paved Warren Turnpike. This is the junction with the A.T. coming north on Warren Turnpike from U.S. 7 bridge. It is the northern terminus of the Mohawk Trail.

Questions and answers about the Appalachian Trail

Preparation

What should I carry?

The A.T. is enjoyable to hike, but inexperienced hikers—even those just out for an hour or two—can quickly find themselves deep in the woods, on steep terrain, and in wet, chilly conditions. Carrying a basic "kit" helps hikers cope with such situations.

Packing for a day-hike is relatively simple:

> Map and compass (learn to use them first!)
> Water (at least 2–3 quarts)
> Warm clothing and rain gear
> Food (including extra high-energy snacks)
> Trowel (to bury human waste) and toilet paper
> First-aid kit, with blister treatments
> Whistle (three blasts is the international signal for help)
> Garbage bag (to carry out trash)

On longer hikes, especially in remote or rugged terrain, add:

> Flashlight (with extra batteries and bulb)
> Heavy-duty garbage bag (emergency shelter or to insulate a hypothermia victim)
> Sharp knife
> Fire starter (a candle, for instance) and waterproof matches

If you're backpacking and plan to camp out, we suggest you consult a good "how-to" book for details about what to carry or talk to an experienced hiker. Although we don't have room here to discuss gear in detail, most A.T. backpackers carry the following items, in addition to the day-hike checklist. Some of the items can be shared with a partner to lighten the load:

> Shelter (a tent or tarp)
> Lightweight pot, cooking utensils
> Stove (a small backpacking model, with fuel)
> Medium-sized backpack (big "expedition-size" packs
> are usually overkill)
> A pack cover or plastic bag (to keep gear dry in rainy weather)
> Sleeping pad (to insulate you from the cold ground)
> Sleeping bag of appropriate warmth for the season
> Food and clothing
> Rope or cord (to hang your food at night)
> Water filter, iodine tablets, or another method of treating water

Where can I park?

Park in designated areas. Many of them will be indicated in the Trailhead entries for this guidebook and may be marked on Trail maps. If you leave your car overnight unattended, however, you risk theft or vandalism. Many hikers avoid this worry by arranging for a "shuttle" (check <www.appalachiantrail.org> for a list) to drop them off at a Trailhead or arranging to leave their car in the parking lot of a business located near the Trail; ask first, and offer to pay a little something to the business. Some sections of the Trail are served by public transportation. If you decide to park at a Trailhead, hide your property and valuables from sight, or, better yet, leave them at home, so they do not inspire a thief to break in and steal them.

Using the Trail

Where and how do I find water?

Year-round natural water sources are listed in this guidebook; springs and streams are marked on most official A.T. maps. Most (although not all) shelters are near a year-round water source. Some springs and streams dry up during late summer and early fall.

Is the water safe to drink?
Water in the backcountry and in water sources along the A.T. can be contaminated by microorganisms, including *giardia lamblia* and others that cause diarrhea or stomach problems. We recommend that you treat all water, using a filter or purifier or water-treatment tablets, or by boiling it.

Are there rest rooms?
Many A.T. shelters have privies, but usually you will need to "go in the woods." Proper disposal of human (and pet) waste is not only a courtesy to other hikers, but a vital Leave No Trace practice for maintaining healthy water supplies in the backcountry and an enjoyable hiking experience for others. No one should venture onto the A.T. without a trowel, used for digging a "cathole" 6"–8" deep to bury waste. Bury feces at least two hundred feet or seventy paces away from water, trails, or shelters. Use a stick to mix dirt with your waste, which hastens decomposition and discourages animals from digging it up. Used toilet paper should either be buried in your cathole or carried out in a sealed plastic bag. Hygiene products such as sanitary napkins should always be carried out.

Can I wash up in a mountain stream or spring?
Please don't. Carry water from the water source in a bottle or other container, and then wash your dishes, and yourself, at least 70 paces away from streams, springs, and ponds. Don't leave food scraps to rot in water sources, and don't foul them with products such as detergent, toothpaste, and human or animal waste.

Are bikes allowed on the Trail?
Only where the Appalachian Trail shares the route with the C&O Towpath in Maryland, the Virginia Creeper Trail in the vicinity of Damascus, Virginia, roads in towns, and on certain bridges. They are not permitted on most of the Trail.

Can I bring my dog?
Yes, except where dogs are prohibited (in Great Smoky Mountains National Park, Bear Mountain Zoo, and Baxter State Park). Dogs must be leashed on National Park Service lands and on many state park and forest lands. ATC's Web site, <www.appalachiantrail.org>, offers details about

hiking with dogs. Although dogs can be wonderful hiking companions, they can create many problems for other hikers and wildlife if you don't control them. If taken, they should not be allowed to run free; leashing at all times is strongly recommended and the law on 40 percent or more of the Trail. Keep dogs out of springs and shelters and away from other hikers, their food, and their gear. Not all dogs can stand the wear and tear of a long hike.

How about horses, llamas, or other pack stock?
Horses are not allowed on the A.T., except where the Appalachian Trail coincides for about three miles with the C&O Canal Towpath in Maryland and on about 50 percent of the A.T. in the Smokies (where, by law, the route is open for horses as a historical use). Llamas and other pack animals are not allowed on the A.T., which is designed, built, and maintained for foot travel. Pack animals would seriously damage the treadway, discourage volunteer maintenance efforts, and make the Trail experience less enjoyable for other hikers.

Are any fees required to hike the A.T.?
No. However, there are entrance fees to some of the national parks the Trail passes through, as well as parking fees and campsite fees in popular areas, to help pay for maintenance costs.

Health and safety

Is the Trail a safe place?
In general, yes. But, like many other popular recreational activities, hiking on the A.T. is not without risk. Don't let the following discussion of potential dangers alarm you or discourage you from enjoying the Trail, but remember not to leave your common sense and intuition behind when you strap on your backpack. Prepare mentally and emotionally.

In an emergency, how do I get help?
Much of the A.T. is within range of cellular phone systems, although signal reception is sometimes not good in gaps, hollows, and valleys; shelters are often located in such areas of poor reception. Emergency

numbers are included in this guidebook and on maps. If you don't have a phone or can't get through, the standard call for distress consists of three short calls, audible or visible, repeated at regular intervals. A whistle is particularly good for audible signals. Visible signals may include, in daytime, light flashed with a mirror or smoke puffs; at night, a flashlight or three small bright fires. Anyone recognizing such a signal should acknowledge with two calls—if possible, by the same method—then go to the distressed person to determine the nature of the emergency. Arrange for additional aid, if necessary.

Most of the A.T. is well-enough traveled that, if you are injured, you can expect to be found. However, if an area is remote and the weather is bad, fewer hikers will be on the Trail, especially after dark. As a rule, keep your pack with you, and, even in an emergency, don't leave marked trails and try to "bushwhack" out—you will be harder to find and are more likely to encounter dangerous terrain. If you must leave the Trail, study the guidebook or map carefully for the nearest place where people are likely to be and attempt to move in that direction. If it is necessary to leave a heavy pack behind, be sure to take essentials, in case your rescue is delayed. In bad weather, a night in the open without proper covering could be fatal.

What's the most dangerous aspect of hiking the A.T.?

Perhaps the most serious dangers are hypothermia (see page 282), a fall on slick rocks and logs, or a sprained or broken limb far from the nearest rescue squad or pay phone. Those are also the best arguments for hiking with a partner, who can get help in an emergency.

What sort of first-aid kit should I pack?

A basic kit to take care of bruises, scrapes, skinned knees, and blisters. The following kit weighs about a pound and occupies about a 3″ x 6″ x 9″ space: eight 4″ x 4″ gauze pads; four 3″ x 4″ gauze pads; five 2″ bandages; ten 1″ bandages; six alcohol prep pads; ten large butterfly closures; one triangular bandage (40″); two 3″ rolls of gauze; twenty tablets of aspirin-free pain-killer; one 15′ roll of 2″ adhesive tape; one 3″ Ace bandage; one 3″ x 4″ moleskin or other blister-care products; three safety pins; one small scissors; one tweezers; personal medications as necessary.

Will I encounter snakes?
Poisonous and nonpoisonous snakes are widespread along the Trail in warm weather, but they will usually be passive. Watch where you step and where you put your hands. Please, don't kill snakes! Some are federally protected under the Endangered Species Act.

What other creatures are problems for people?
Allergic reactions to bee stings can be a problem. Ticks, which carry Lyme disease, are also a risk; always check yourself for ticks daily. Poisonous spiders are sometimes found at shelters and campsites. Mosquitoes and blackflies may plague you in some seasons. Porcupines, skunks, raccoons, and squirrels are quite common and occasionally raid shelters and well-established camping areas after dark, looking for food. Mice are permanent residents at most shelters and may carry diseases.

What about bears?
Black bears live along most parts of the Trail and are particularly common in Georgia, the Shenandoah and Great Smoky Mountains national parks, and parts of Pennsylvania and New Jersey. They are always looking for food. Bears that have lost their fear of humans may "bluff charge" to get you to drop food or a backpack. If you encounter a black bear, it will probably run away. If it does not, back away slowly, watching the bear but not making direct eye contact. Do not run away or play dead. If a bear attacks, fight for all you are worth. The best defense against bears is preparing and storing food properly. Cook and eat your meals away from your tent or shelter, so food odors do not linger. Hang your food, cookware, toothpaste, and personal-hygiene items in a sturdy bag from a strong tree branch at least ten feet off the ground, four feet from the tree and branch, and well away from your campsite.

Is poison ivy common along the A.T.?
Yes. It grows plentifully in the wild, particularly south of New England, and can be an annoyance during hiking season. If you have touched poison ivy, wash immediately with strong soap (but not with one containing added oil). If a rash develops in the next day or so, treat it with calamine lotion or Solarcaine. Do not scratch. If blisters become serious or the rash spreads to the eyes, see a doctor.

Will I catch a disease?

The most common illnesses encountered on the A.T. are water-borne, come from ingesting protozoa (such as *giardia lamblia*), and respond well to antibiotics. But, the Lyme-disease bacterium and other tick-borne illnesses are legitimate concerns, too; mosquito-borne illnesses such as the West Nile virus are less common in Trail states. Cases of rabies have been reported in foxes, raccoons, and other small animals; a bite is a serious concern, although instances of hikers being bitten are rare. One case of the dangerous rodent-borne disease hantavirus has been reported on the A.T.: Avoid sleeping on mouse droppings (use a mat or tent) or handling mice. Treat your water, and wash your hands.

Will I encounter hazardous weather?

Walking in the open means you will be susceptible to sudden changes in the weather, and traveling on foot means that it may be hard to find shelter quickly. Pay attention to the changing skies. Sudden spells of "off-season" cold weather, hail, and even snow are common along many parts of the Trail. Winter-like weather often occurs in late spring or early fall in the southern Appalachians, Vermont, New Hampshire, and Maine. In the northern Appalachians, it can snow during any month of the year.

What are the most serious weather-related dangers?

Hypothermia, lightning, and heat exhaustion are all legitimate concerns. Don't let the fear of them ruin your hike, but take sensible precautions.

Hypothermia—A cold rain can be the most dangerous weather of all, because it can cause hypothermia (or "exposure") even when conditions are well above freezing. Hypothermia occurs when wind and rain chill the body so that its core temperature drops; death occurs if the condition is not caught in time. Avoid hypothermia by dressing in layers of synthetic clothing, eating well, staying hydrated, and knowing when to hole up in a warm sleeping bag in a tent or shelter. Cotton clothing, such as blue jeans, tends to chill you when it gets wet from rain or sweat; if the weather turns bad, cotton clothes increase your risk of hypothermia. Natural wool and artificial fibers such as nylon, polyester, and polypropylene all do a much better job of insulation in cold, wet weather. Remember that, when the wind blows, its "chill" effect can make you

TEMPERATURE (¼F)

WIND (mph)	40	35	30	25	20	15	10	5	0	-5	-10	-15	-20	-25	-30	-35	-40	-45
5	36	31	25	19	13	7	1	-5	-11	-16	-22	-28	-34	-40	-46	-52	-57	-63
10	34	27	21	15	9	3	-4	-10	-16	-22	-28	-35	-41	-47	-53	-59	-66	-72
15	32	25	19	13	6	0	-7	-13	-19	-26	-32	-39	-45	-51	-58	-64	-71	-77
20	30	24	17	11	4	-2	-9	-15	-22	-29	-35	-42	-48	-55	-61	-68	-74	-81
25	29	23	16	9	3	-4	-11	-17	-24	-31	-37	-44	-51	-58	-64	-71	-78	-84
30	28	22	15	8	1	-5	-12	-19	-26	-33	-39	-46	-53	-60	-67	-73	-80	-87
35	28	21	14	7	0	-7	-14	-21	-27	-34	-41	-48	-55	-62	-69	-76	-82	-89
40	27	20	13	6	-1	-8	-15	-22	-29	-36	-43	-50	-57	-64	-71	-78	-84	-91
45	26	19	12	5	-2	-9	-16	-23	-30	-37	-44	-51	-58	-65	-72	-79	-86	-93
50	26	19	12	4	-3	-10	-17	-24	-31	-38	-45	-52	-60	-67	-74	-81	-88	-95
55	25	18	11	4	-3	-11	-18	-25	-32	-39	-46	-54	-61	-68	-75	-82	-89	-97
60	25	17	10	3	-4	-11	-19	-26	-33	-40	-48	-55	-62	-69	-76	-84	-91	-98

30 min.   10 min.   5 minutes

FROSTBITE TIMES

Wind Chill (¼F) = $35.74 + 0.6215T - 35.75(V^{0.16}) + 0.4275T(V^{0.16})$
Where, T= Air Temperature (¼F)   V= Wind Speed (mph)
National Weather Service and National Oceanic and Atmospheric Administration
Effective 11/01/01

much colder than the temperature would lead you to suspect, especially if you're sweaty or wet.

Lightning—The odds of being struck by lightning are low, but an open ridge is no place to be during a thunderstorm. If a storm is coming, immediately leave exposed areas. Boulders, rocky overhangs, and shallow caves offer no protection from lightning, which may actually flow through them along the ground after a strike. Tents and convertible automobiles are no good, either. Sheltering in hard-roofed automobiles or large buildings is best, although they are rarely available to the hiker. Avoid tall structures, such as ski lifts, flagpoles, power-line towers, and the tallest trees, solitary rocks, or open hilltops. If you cannot enter a building or car, take shelter in a stand of smaller trees or in the forest. Avoid clearings. If caught in the open, crouch down on your pack or pad, or roll into a ball. If you are in water, get out. Disperse groups, so that not everyone is struck by a single bolt. Do not hold a potential lightning rod, such as a fishing pole or metal hiking pole.

Dehydration—Dry, hot summers are common along the Trail, particularly in the Virginias and the mid-Atlantic. Water may be scarce on humid days, sweat does not evaporate well, and many hikers face the danger of heat stroke and heat exhaustion if they haven't taken proper precautions, such as drinking lots of water. Learn how to protect yourself from heat exhaustion. Dehydration also is common in winter, when sweating may not be as obvious. Drink lots of water all year!

Is crime a problem?

The Appalachian Trail is safer than most places, but a few crimes of violence have occurred. Awareness is one of your best lines of defense. Be aware of what you are doing, where you are, and to whom you are talking. Hikers looking out for each other can be an effective "community watch." Be prudent and cautious without allowing common sense to slip into paranoia. Remember to trust your gut—it's usually right. Other tips include the following:

- Don't hike alone. If you are by yourself and encounter a stranger who makes you feel uncomfortable, say you are with a group that is behind you. Be creative. If in doubt, move on. Even a partner is no guarantee of safety, however; pay attention to your instincts about other people.

- Leave your hiking itinerary and timetable with someone at home, but don't post it on an on-line Trail journal. Be sure your contacts and your family know your "Trail name," if you use one of those fanciful aliases common on the A.T. Check in regularly, and establish a procedure to follow if you fail to check in. On short hikes, provide your contacts with the numbers of the land-managing agencies for the area of your hike. On extended hikes, provide ATC's number, (304) 535-6331.

- Be wary of strangers. Be friendly, but cautious. Don't tell strangers your plans (and don't post them in real time on the Internet). Avoid people who act suspiciously, seem hostile, or are intoxicated.

- Don't camp near roads.

- Dress conservatively to avoid unwanted attention.

- Don't carry firearms. With appropriate state permits, possession of them (but not their discharge) is permitted on federal lands, but they could be turned against you or result in an accidental shooting, and they are extra weight. Veteran hikers affirm they are not necessary. (Hunting regulations are different and vary by land ownership.)

- Eliminate opportunities for theft. Don't bring jewelry. Hide your money. If you must leave your pack, hide it, or leave it with someone trustworthy. Don't leave valuables or equipment (especially in sight) in vehicles parked at Trailheads.

- Use the Trail registers (the notebooks stored at most shelters). Sign in using your given name, leave a note, and report any suspicious activities. If someone needs to locate you, or if a serious crime has been committed along the Trail, the first place authorities will look is in the registers.

- Report any crime or harassment to the local authorities and ATC (at <incident@appalachiantrail.org>).

Trail history

Who was Benton MacKaye, and what was his connection to the Appalachian Trail?

He first published the idea. MacKaye (1879–1975) grew up mostly in Shirley Center, Massachusetts, reading the work of American naturalists and poets and taking long walks in the mountains of Massachusetts and Vermont. MacKaye (which is pronounced like "sky") sometimes claimed that the idea for the A.T. was born one day when he was sitting in a tree atop Stratton Mountain in Vermont. After graduating from Harvard, he eventually went to work in the new U.S. Forest Service and began carving out a niche as a profound thinker and an advocate for wilderness. By 1919, his radical ideas had led to him being edged out of the government, and he turned his attention to creating a new discipline that later came to be called "regional planning." His initial 1921 "project in regional planning" was a proposal for a network of work camps and communities in the mountains, all linked by a trail that ran from the highest point in New England to the highest point in the South. He called it "an Appalachian Trail."

Why did he propose it?
MacKaye was convinced that the pace of urban and industrial life along the East Coast was harmful to people. He envisioned the A.T. as a path interspersed with planned wilderness communities where people could go to renew themselves. That idea never gained much traction, but the notion of a two-thousand-mile footpath in the mountains fired the imaginations of hikers and outdoorsmen from Maine to Georgia. Inspired by him, they began building trails and trying to connect them.

What was his connection to the Appalachian Trail Conference?
MacKaye was responsible for convening and organizing the first Appalachian Trail "conference" in Washington, D.C., in 1925. That gathering of hikers, foresters, and public officials embraced the goal of building the Trail. They established the Appalachian Trail Conference, appointed MacKaye as its "field organizer," and named Major William Welch, manager of New York's Harriman Park, as its first chairman.

What happened next?
Perfunctory scouting of routes took place. A few short sections were marked and connected. New trails were built in New York. Welch designed a logo and Trail markers. Committees met in northeastern states and talked about the idea. But, for several years, the idea didn't really go anywhere. MacKaye was much better at inspirational abstract thinking than practical organizing, and it soon became apparent that someone else was going to have to take the lead for the Trail to actually get built.

Who pushed the project forward?
Two men, retired Judge Arthur Perkins of Connecticut and admiralty lawyer Myron H. Avery of Washington, D.C. Perkins took the idea and ran with it, essentially appointing himself as the acting chairman of ATC in the late 1920s and recruiting Avery to lead the effort in the area around Washington. Both began vigorously proselytizing the idea of the Trail in 1928 and 1929, championing MacKaye's ideas to recruit volunteers,

establishing hiking clubs up and down the coast, and actually going out to hike, clear brush, and mark paths themselves. As Perkins' health failed in the early 1930s, Avery took over, devoting incredible time, energy, and willpower to establishing a network of volunteers, developing clubs, working with the government, building the organization of the ATC, and setting the Trail's northern terminus at Katahdin in his native Maine. Avery remained chairman of ATC until 1952.

What was the relationship between MacKaye and Myron Avery?
They were cordial at first, but, by the mid-1930s, as Avery took charge of the Trail project, they quarreled over fundamental issues and visions of what the Trail should be. Avery was more interested in hiking and in connecting the sections of the Trail, while MacKaye was more interested in the Trail's role in promoting wilderness protection.

When was the Trail completed?
In 1937. It fell into disrepair during World War II, when Trail maintainers were unable to work on it, and parts of the route were lost. After the war, a concerted effort was made to restore it, and it was once again declared complete in 1951.

What happened after it was completed?
It's useful to look at the Trail's history in three eras: the era of Trail-building, which lasted until the Trail was completed in 1937; the era of Trail protection, which lasted until 1968, when Congress made the A.T. a national scenic trail; and the era of management and promotion, which has lasted until the present day. The first era was dominated by personalities and focused on getting the thing built and blazed from one end to the other. The second era saw the beginning of growth of the clubs taking care of it and the Conference, the construction of shelters, and a continuing battle to keep the route open over the many hundreds of miles of private property that it crossed. The third era saw an explosion of the number of people hiking the A.T. as the government began buying land along the route to guarantee the permanence of the footpath and volunteers shifted their emphasis to the hard work of managing a part of the national park system. In July 2005, the Conference became the A.T. Conservancy, to better express its work of protecting Trail resources.

How was the original Trail different from today's A.T.?

At first, the goal was simply to blaze a connected route. Often, this meant that the Trail led along old forest roads and other trails. Trail maintainers mostly just cleared brush and painted blazes. Today's Trail has mostly been moved off the old roads and onto new paths dug and reinforced especially for hikers. Today's route, although engineered much more elaborately, often requires more climbing, because it leads up the sides of many mountains that the old woods roads bypassed.

How do terms like "Trailway," "greenway," "buffer," and "viewshed" fit into this history?

The idea of a "Trailway" was first embraced by ATC in 1937. It meant that there was more to the Appalachian Trail than just the footpath. The "Trailway" referred to an area dedicated to the interests of those on foot, originally a mile on either side. In some cases, that came to mean a "buffer"—a legally protected area around the path that kept the sights and sounds of civilization, logging, and development away from the solitary hiker. In other cases, it meant a great deal more. It evolved into a notion of a "greenway," a broad swath of protected land through which the Trail ran. Crucial to the idea of a greenway was that of the "viewshed," the countryside visible from the Trail's high points. In the years since the A.T. became a national scenic trail, the Conservancy has worked to influence the development of surrounding areas so that the views from the Trail remain scenic, even when those views are of areas well outside the boundaries of the public Trail lands themselves.

When did Trail protection begin?

The notion of a protected zone was first formalized in an October 15, 1938, agreement between the National Park Service and the U.S. Forest Service for the promotion of an Appalachian Trailway through the relevant national parks and forests, extending one mile on each side of the Trail. Within this zone, no new parallel roads would be built or any other incompatible development allowed. Timber cutting would not be permitted within 200 feet of the Trail. Similar agreements, creating a zone one-quarter-mile in width, were signed with most states through which the Trail passes.

How were Trail lands identified?

Much of the Trail was already in national forests or national parks and state and local parks, but large portions were on private property, with the agreement of the property owners. In 1970, supplemental agreements under the 1968 National Trails Systems Act—among the National Park Service, the U.S. Forest Service, and the Appalachian Trail Conservancy—established the specific responsibilities of those organizations for initial mapping, selection of rights-of-way, relocations, maintenance, development, acquisition of land, and protection of a permanent Trail. Agreements also were signed between the Park Service and the various states, encouraging them to acquire and protect a right-of-way.

Why has complete protection taken so long?

Getting federal money appropriated was difficult, and not all property owners were willing to sell, which occasionally raised the specter of the government's threatening to condemn land for the Trail—always a politically unpopular action. Slow progress of federal efforts and lack of initiative by some states led Congress to strengthen the National Trails System Act in an amendment known as the Appalachian Trail Bill, which was signed by President Jimmy Carter on March 21, 1978. The new legislation emphasized the need for protecting the Trail, including acquiring a corridor, and authorized $90 million for that purpose. More money was appropriated during the Reagan, Bush, and Clinton administrations. Today, more than 99 percent of the Trail runs across public lands.

What is the relationship between the A.T. and the government, the Conservancy, and the clubs?

In 1984, the Interior Department delegated the responsibility for managing the A.T. corridor lands outside established parks and forests to the ATC. The Conservancy and its affiliated clubs retain primary responsibility for maintaining the footpath, too. A more comprehensive, 10-year agreement was signed in 1994 and renewed in November 2004.

Trail geology

The geological underpinnings of the Appalachian Trail are best described in *Underfoot: A Geologic Guide to the Appalachian Trail*, by V. Collins Chew, referred to throughout this guidebook and available from the Ultimate A.T. Store (888-AT STORE or <www.atctrailstore.org>.)

Wildlife along the A.T.

How "wild" is the A.T.?

The well-known plaque at Springer Mountain in Georgia describes the A.T. as "a footpath for those who seek fellowship with the wilderness." What does that mean? The Trail will indeed take you deep into some of the wildest and most remote woodlands of the eastern United States. But, true "wilderness," in the sense of untouched wild country, is rare, even on the A.T. Much of the land that the Trail follows was once farmland—even the steep, stony, remote slopes—and nearly all of it has been logged at some time during the last four centuries. Except for bears, bobcats, and coyotes, most large natural predators have been exterminated.

In the twentieth century, much of the formerly settled land was incorporated into state and national parks and forests. On that land, forests and wildlife have returned. As you walk through what seems like primeval wilderness, you're likely to run across old stone walls or abandoned logging roads or the foundations of nineteenth-century homesteads. The federal government has designated some of those areas as protected wilderness areas, which strictly limits the ways in which they can be used. Today, the mountains teem with creatures of all sorts, from microbes to moose. To the casual hiker who knows only the woods of a suburban park, it can seem very wild indeed.

One good way to look at the "wilderness" of the A.T. is as a series of long, skinny islands of wildness, surrounded by a sea of populated valleys inhabited by working farms and suburban communities. In the vast national forests of the South and the spreading timberlands of northern New England, those "islands" are somewhat broader. But, even in its wildest places, the A.T. hiker is rarely more than a strenuous day's walk from the nearest highway or community.

What large animals might I see?

Moose, the largest animal that hikers encounter along the Trail (often weighing in at more than 1,000 pounds), inhabit deep woodlands and wetlands from Massachusetts north, especially in New Hampshire and Maine. White-tailed deer can be found along the entire length of the Trail. Elk have been reintroduced to Pennsylvania, North Carolina, and Tennessee. Black bears have been spotted in all Trail states and are especially common in Georgia, North Carolina, Tennessee, Virginia, Pennsylvania, and New Jersey. Wild boars live in the Great Smoky Mountains National Park. Bobcats and coyotes are stealthy residents along most of the route of the Trail, although they're rarely seen. Fishers, otters, and beavers are occasionally reported by hikers.

What small animals might I see?

By far the most familiar will be mice, chipmunks, rabbits, and squirrels, but foxes, raccoons, opossums, skunks, groundhogs, porcupines, bats, weasels, shrews, minks, and muskrats are also common. Tree frogs and bullfrogs inhabit wet areas in warm weather, lizards scurry along rocks and fallen logs, snakes (both venomous and not) are common south of New England, and streams and ponds are home to salamanders, bass, trout, bream, sunfish, and crayfish.

Which animals are dangerous?

Few A.T. hikers encounter aggressive animals, but any wild animal will fight if cornered or handled roughly—even timid animals such as deer can be quite dangerous in those circumstances. The large wild animals most likely to be aggressive include moose (during rutting season) and black bears (especially mother bears with cubs). Mountain lions, which have stalked people in western states, have long been rumored to have returned to the Appalachians, but so far scientists have not been able to confirm any sightings in mountains that the A.T. traverses.

When disturbed or stepped on, many other creatures will strike back aggressively, inflicting painful wounds or poisonous stings. Those include timber rattlesnakes and copperheads, hornets, wasps, yellow jackets, Africanized bees, and black widow and brown recluse spiders. Foxes, bats, raccoons, and other small animals susceptible to rabies may bite when suffering from infection. Mice, although not aggressive, may transmit diseases, and biting insects such as mosquitoes and ticks can infect hikers with bacteria. Hikers in more populated sections of the Trail also might encounter aggressive dogs.

What rare or endangered animal species might I see?

Birders might spot rare species such as the Bicknell's thrush, hermit thrush, gray-cheeked thrush, northern raven, olive-sided flycatcher, black-billed cuckoo, spruce grouse, bay-breasted warbler, cerulean warbler, blackburnian warbler, magnolia warbler, blackpoll warbler, alder flycatcher, rusty blackbird, Swainson's warbler, yellow-bellied sapsucker, winter wren, red-breasted nuthatch, sharp-shinned hawk, northern saw-whet owl, golden eagle, peregrine falcon, merlin, bald eagle, and Cooper's hawk.

Harder to find, but also present, are the Carolina northern flying squirrel, Virginia northern flying squirrel, rock vole, Allegheny wood rat, eastern wood rat, water shrew, and fence lizard. The black bear and eastern timber rattlesnake, although not uncommon along the Trail, are on the rare-species list. You may also find a number of rare crustaceans, reptiles, and amphibians, including the zig-zag salamander, northern cricket frog, triangle floater mussel, Jefferson salamander, Appalachian brook crayfish, wood turtle, broadhead skink, pigmy salamander, shovelnose salamander, Shenandoah salamander, Weller's salamander, and squawfoot mussel.

What birds will I see in the Appalachians that I might not see at my backyard feeder?

Birds with summer ranges normally far to the north of where most A.T. hikers live are often found in the mountains, where the altitude makes the climate resemble that of Canada. Insect-eating birds such as whip-poorwills, flycatchers, and swallows rarely show up in backyards but are common along the Trail. The songs of deep-woods birds such as the ovenbird, kinglet, veery, pewee, and red-eyed vireo will provide an ongoing chorus for summer hikers. Pileated woodpeckers hammer deliberately on dead trees. Large game birds, such as wild turkey, ruffed grouse, and spruce grouse, forage on the forest floor and surprise hikers as they burst into flight. Many hikers linger to admire the soaring acrobatics of ravens, vultures, hawks, eagles, and falcons on the thermals and updrafts along the rocky crests of the mountains.

Trees and wild plants along the A.T.

How old are the Appalachian forests?

The forests of the Appalachians have been logged heavily for more than three centuries. Photographs from the late nineteenth and early twentieth centuries show many areas almost completely stripped of trees. Many Trail areas were open farmland or pastureland in the 1700s and early 1800s. Lumber is still harvested in national forests and privately owned timberlands along the Trail. Although today's mountains are heavily forested again, it is mostly "second-growth" timber, except in a few isolated coves of "old-growth" forest that date back to precolonial times.

Forest that has grown back from burning or clearing through successive stages to the point at which it reaches a fairly steady state, with dominant full-grown trees, is known as a "climax forest." Several different climax forests appear along the A.T., and they are not mutually exclusive—different types can be found on the same mountain. The kind you encounter will depend on where you are, on what type of soil is underfoot, and the climate. The climate often depends on how high the mountains are—the higher they are, the more "northern" (or boreal) the climate.

What kinds of forests will I encounter along the Trail?

■ The mixed deciduous forest (also called the southern hardwood forest) dominates the foothills of the southern mountains and Trail lands south of New England. Various kinds of broad-leafed trees are dominant, and the understory of small trees and shrubs is profuse. Oak and hickory are the most common large trees, with maple and beech evident in more northerly sections; some sproutings of chestnut (a species that dominated until a blight devastated it early in the twentieth century) can be found as well. Understory trees such as redbud, dogwood, striped maple, and American holly are common, as are shrubs such as witch hazel, pawpaw, and mountain pepperbush.

■ The southern Appalachian forest, found above the foothills from Georgia to Massachusetts-Connecticut, contains more tree species than any other forest in North America and actually takes in a range of different forest types that can vary dramatically according to elevation. Climax hardwood forests of basswood, birch, maple, beech, tuliptree, ash, and magnolia can be found in some coves, while, above about 4,000 feet, the climax forests are typically spruce, fir, and hemlock, particularly on the wetter western slopes. Old-growth forest can be found in isolated parts of the Great Smoky Mountains National Park. Oak forests often predominate on the eastern faces of the mountains, which typically do not receive as much moisture. Pine and oak may mix on some slopes. At higher elevations, the understory is less varied: Shrubs of mountain laurel and rhododendron form nearly impenetrable thickets that are densest where conditions are wettest.

■ The transition forest tends to be wetter and more northerly than the mixed deciduous forest. Hikers marveling at the colors of a New England fall are admiring the transition forest. It extends across the hillsides and lowlands of the north and reaches down into the high country of the southern Appalachians. It appears as a mosaic of spruce, fir, hemlock, pine, birch, maple, basswood, and beech forests. The substory of transition forest tends to be more open, with ferns and shrubs of elderberry, hazel, and bush honeysuckle, and often a thick carpet of evergreen needles covers the ground under the trees. Conifers tend to predominate at the higher elevations.

■ The northern, or boreal forest, is the largest North American forest. Most of it is in Canada and Alaska, but A.T. hikers encounter it while traversing the highest ridges of the southern Appalachians and the coniferous uplands of northern New England. Pines and hemlocks characterize its southern reaches, while dwarfed spruces and firs (known as krummholz or taiga) grow at treeline in New Hampshire and Maine, just as they grow at the borders of the arctic lands farther north. In between is a spruce-fir climax forest. Evergreens such as white pine, red pine, white spruce, balsam fir, black spruce, and jack pine predominate, but hardwoods such as aspen and birch are mixed in as well. The ground of the boreal forest is typically thin and muddy, with little in the way of an understory, and it includes sphagnum bogs surrounded by a wide variety of aquatic plants, ferns, subalpine plants, blueberry bushes, and mountain maple and ash shrubs.

What wildflowers can I look for, and when will I see them?
Among the small joys of hiking the Trail are the wildflowers that grow along the way. Some poke their heads out of the forest duff in late winter and are gone by the time the spreading canopy of late-spring trees blocks out the sun. Some cluster near the edges of clearings in midsummer, while others hide in the deep shade. And, still others blossom amid the falling leaves and early snows of the Appalachian fall.

Winter/early spring—First to bloom in swampy areas most years is the maroon-colored cowl that shelters the tiny, foul-smelling flowers of skunk cabbage, which may appear while snow is still on the ground. In March and April, along the high, dry ridges, the delicate starbursts of bloodroot appear, along with the corncob-like clusters of squaw root on fallen oak trees; the graceful, lily-like dogtooth violet; the white bunches of early saxifrage; fanlike, purple clusters of dwarf iris in southern sections; the pink-purple flowers and liver-shaped leaves of hepatica; the delicate, white rue anemone; the bee-buzzing carpets of fringed phacelia in the South; and the waxy, pink trailing arbutus farther north.

Spring/early summer—During May and June, as the tree canopy shades the forest floor, the variety of wildflowers blooming along the A.T. becomes too extensive to keep track of. The bubblegum scent and orange blooms of flame azalea shrubs burst out in the southern Appalachians, along with the white and pink blossoms of its close relatives, mountain laurel and rhododendron. The garlicky wild leek, or ramp, flowers in early summer. Hikers may spot the green tubes of jack-in-the-pulpit, dove-like red clusters of wild columbine, vessel-like orchid blossoms of pink lady's-slipper, spade-leaved trillium, bright blue of viper's bugloss, the blue-violet of spiderwort in sunny clearings, black cohosh's delicate cone of tiny blooms, and, in the cold bogs of the northern states, the white blossoms of Labrador tea and the pink pentagons of bog laurel.

Late summer—The heat of July and August in the Appalachians coaxes blossoms from a number of mountain shrubs, shade plants, and meadow plants. Wintergreen blooms white in oak forests, the white starbursts of tall meadow rue appear near open fields, the white petals of the bug-trapping sundew appear in wet areas, mountain cranberry's small bell-like pink blossoms appear in New England, the white-and-yellow sunbursts of oxeye daisy grow along hedgerows, and the greenish-white clusters of wild sarsaparilla appear in the dry, open woods. In the mid-Atlantic states, the understory becomes a waist-deep sea of wood nettle, the delicate white flowers of which belie unpleasant stinging hairs that bristle from the stems and leaves. The succulent stalks of jewel-weed, which has a pale yellow-and-orange flower, often sprout nearby, and their juice can help ease the sting and itch of the nettles and poison ivy.

Fall and early winter—Certain wildflowers continue blooming late into the fall along the A.T., disappearing from the woods about the same time hikers do. Goldenrod spreads across open fields in September, about the time the leaves start changing color. The intricate white discs of Queen Anne's lace adorn ditches and roadsides until late in the year. Other common fall wildflowers include aster, wood sorrel, monkshood, and butter-and-eggs.

Can I eat wild plants I find?

You could eat certain plants, but, in keeping with the principles of Leave No Trace, you shouldn't. Leave the wild blueberries and raspberries and blackberries of summer for the birds and bears. Resist the temptation to spice up your noodles with ramps in the spring. "Chicken of the woods" mushrooms should stay in the woods. Wild watercress belongs in a stream, not a salad. Rather than brewing your own ginseng or sassafras tea from wild roots, visit the supermarket in town. Many edible plants along the A.T. are rare and endangered, and harvesting them is illegal. Even when the flora are plentiful, remember that the fauna of the Appalachians have no option other than to forage for it; you do.

What rare or endangered plant species might I see?

Most of the federally listed plant species (threatened or endangered) along the Appalachian Trail are found in the high country of the southern Appalachians or the alpine environments of northern New England. There are too many to list here, but typical of those in the southern Appalachians is the spreading avens, a plant with fan-shaped leaves and small, yellow flowers that grows in rock crevices. Although bluets are common along the A.T., a subspecies called Roan Mountain bluet is found in only nine sites there—the only known sites in the world. Gray's lily is found only on the high balds near Roan Mountain. Although goldenrod is plentiful along the Trail and sometimes considered something of a pest, one rare subspecies, the Blue Ridge goldenrod, is known to exist only on one cliff in North Carolina. Similarly, many of the plants at and above treeline in New England, such as Robbins cinquefoil, are extremely vulnerable to damage from hikers wandering off the A.T. Below treeline, plants such as the small whorled pogonia, an orchid, are threatened by development. Please don't pick the flowers along the A.T.—they might be the only ones of a kind.

The how and why of Trail construction

Who decides which route the Trail takes?

A local Trail-maintaining club, in consultation with the Appalachian Trail Conservancy and the government agency responsible for managing the land in question, determines the route that the footpath follows over a section. According to the National Trails System Act that authorized federal protection of the A.T., the goal is to expose the walker to "the maximum outdoor recreation potential and … enjoyment of the nationally significant scenic, historic, natural, or cultural qualities of the area." In plain language, that means routing the Trail in such a way that walkers have the chance to encounter and appreciate the wildlife, geography, and geology, as well as the historical and natural context of the Appalachians, while merging with, exploring, and harmonizing with the mountain environment.

How is today's A.T. different from the original Trail?

When the A.T. was first built, the main goal was a continuous, marked route, which often meant connecting existing footpaths and woods roads. Long sections of "roadwalks" linked the footpaths. Where no existing routes were available, Trail builders marked out new ones, cleared brush, and painted blazes. But, that was about it, and, for many years, when few people knew about or hiked the Trail, it was enough. Beginning in the 1960s, two things happened: The A.T. became a part of the national park system, and the numbers of people using it began skyrocketing. With increased use, mud and erosion became problems. As the Trail was moved away from existing footpaths and roads and onto new paths planned and built especially for the A.T. on federal land, Trail builders began "hardening" the path and designing it to stand up to heavier use.

What causes the Trail to deteriorate?

Erosion can damage the footpath quickly. The mineral soil of the footpath is made of very fine particles bound together by clay that, once broken from the ground by boots and hiking poles, is easily washed away by fast-flowing water. (Water moving at two miles per hour has sixty-four times more ability to carry soil particles than water moving at one mile per hour.) Trail builders work to separate water from the treadway. Where that is not possible, they try to slow it down. Since water in rivulets or ruts flows faster than water flowing across the Trail in sheets, trail builders try to channel water off the part that hikers walk on. Where they can't, they slant the path outward so that water will stay "thin" and flow slowly off the sides in a sheet, rather than becoming "thick" and channeling down the middle of the Trail.

Why are parts of the Trail routed over narrow log walkways?

Believe it or not, it's not to keep your feet dry. The goal is to protect the land, not your nice, new boots. Bog bridges, also called "puncheon," allow the Trail to take hikers into an important part of the mountain environment without turning such ecologically sensitive swamp areas into hopeless quagmires, disrupting plant and animal life there. The Trail is supposed to "wear lightly on the land," and this is one way to do so. Walkways may be built on piles driven into the ground, or they may "float" on boggy ground; in both cases, the wetlands are disturbed much less than they would be by mud holes that widen every time a hiker tries to skirt the edges.

Why does the Trail zigzag up steep mountains?

When it was first marked, the Trail often climbed steep slopes by the most direct route, and older parts of today's Trail still tend to have the steepest sections. But, water runs faster down a steeper trail and erodes it more quickly. In recent years, many sections have been rerouted so that the Trail ascends by way of "sidehill" that slants up a mountainside and "switchbacks" that zigzag across its steepest faces. Again, it isn't done to make the Trail easier for hikers, although that's sometimes the effect, but rather to make the footpath itself more durable and less subject to erosion.

How does the Trail cross creeks and rivers?
Bridges take the Trail across all its major river crossings, except for the Kennebec River in Maine (where hikers ferry across in canoes). Most, such as the Bear Mountain Bridge across the Hudson in New York, are highway bridges; a few others, such as the James River Foot Bridge in Virginia, are built especially for foot travelers. A few large creeks require fording, but most are crossed by footbridges or stepping stones. Small streams may require fording when spring floods submerge the rocks and stepping stones that lead across them.

Why are there so many logs and rock barriers in the path?
Unless the logs result from a "blowdown" (a fallen tree) or the rocks from a rockslide, they're probably water-diversion devices, such as waterbars or check dams that have been added to older, eroding sections of the Trail. Avoid stepping on them, if possible: Not only can they be slippery (particularly the logs), but they will last longer if you step over them.

Why is the Trail so rocky?
As you may have read in the section of this guide devoted to geology, the Appalachians are the product of erosion, which tends to strip away soil and leave rocks on the surface. Since rocky sections offer a durable surface and often provide spectacular views for hikers, Trail designers don't hesitate to route the footpath along them. This is particularly true from Massachusetts-Connecticut through Connecticut and eastern New Hampshire through Maine; many older sections of the Trail are routed along ridgelines. Typically, the A.T. will climb a ridge on smoother "sidehill" Trail and then follow a rocky ridgeline for some distance, before descending again.

Summary of distances

<table>
<tr><th colspan="2">North–South</th><th></th><th colspan="2">South–North</th></tr>
<tr><th>From Vermont Line</th><th>Within Section</th><th></th><th>Within Section</th><th>From New York Line</th></tr>
<tr><td colspan="5" align="center">**Massachusetts Section One**</td></tr>
<tr><td>0.0</td><td>0.0</td><td>Vermont–Massachusetts Line</td><td>4.1</td><td>142.0</td></tr>
<tr><td>0.8</td><td>0.8</td><td>Eph's Lookout</td><td>3.3</td><td>141.2</td></tr>
<tr><td>1.3</td><td>1.3</td><td>Pine Cobble Trail</td><td>2.8</td><td>140.7</td></tr>
<tr><td>2.3</td><td>2.3</td><td>Sherman Brook Primitive Campsite</td><td>1.8</td><td>139.7</td></tr>
<tr><td>4.1</td><td>4.1</td><td>Mass. 2 (650')</td><td>0.0</td><td>137.9</td></tr>
<tr><td colspan="5" align="center">**Massachusetts Section Two**</td></tr>
<tr><td>4.1</td><td>0.0</td><td>Mass. 2 (650')</td><td>14.0</td><td>137.9</td></tr>
<tr><td>5.0</td><td>0.9</td><td>Pattison Road</td><td>13.1</td><td>137.0</td></tr>
<tr><td>7.1</td><td>3.0</td><td>Wilbur Clearing Shelter (2,300') side trail</td><td>11.0</td><td>134.9</td></tr>
<tr><td>7.2</td><td>3.1</td><td>Notch Road</td><td>10.9</td><td>134.8</td></tr>
<tr><td>10.4</td><td>6.3</td><td>Mt. Greylock, Bascom Lodge</td><td>7.7</td><td>131.6</td></tr>
<tr><td>10.9</td><td>6.8</td><td>Notch Road, Rockwell Road</td><td>7.2</td><td>131.1</td></tr>
<tr><td>13.1</td><td>9.0</td><td>Jones Nose Trail</td><td>5.0</td><td>128.9</td></tr>
<tr><td>13.7</td><td>9.6</td><td>Mark Noepel Shelter (2,800') side trail</td><td>4.4</td><td>128.3</td></tr>
<tr><td>14.6</td><td>10.5</td><td>Old Adams Road</td><td>3.5</td><td>127.4</td></tr>
<tr><td>17.3</td><td>13.2</td><td>Outlook Avenue</td><td>0.8</td><td>124.7</td></tr>
<tr><td>18.1</td><td>14.0</td><td>Mass. 8 (1,000'), Cheshire, Mass.</td><td>0.0</td><td>123.9</td></tr>
</table>

North–South			**South–North**	
From Vermont Line	*Within Section*		*Within Section*	**From New York Line**

Massachusetts Section Three

18.1	0.0	Mass. 8 (1,000'), Cheshire, Mass.	9.3	123.9
18.6	0.5	Church Street	8.8	123.4
19.8	1.7	The Cobbles side trail	7.6	122.2
22.3	4.2	Gore Pond (2,050')	5.1	119.7
22.7	4.6	Crystal Mountain Campsite	4.7	119.3
26.4	8.3	Gulf Road	1.0	115.6
27.4	9.3	Mass. 8, Mass. 9 (1,200')	0.0	114.6

Massachusetts Section Four

27.4	0.0	Mass. 8, Mass. 9 (1,200')	9.6	114.6
28.0	0.6	CSX Railroad	9.0	114.0
30.1	2.7	Grange Hall Road	6.9	111.9
30.4	3.0	Kay Wood Shelter side trail	6.6	111.6
33.1	5.7	Warner Hill (2,050')	3.9	108.9
33.8	6.4	Blotz Road	3.2	108.2
37.0	9.6	Pittsfield Road	0.0	105.0

Massachusetts Section Five

37.0	0.0	Pittsfield Road	9.4	105.0
38.5	1.5	West Branch Road	7.9	103.5
39.2	2.2	October Mountain Shelter side trail (1,950')	7.2	102.8
40.8	3.8	Bald Top	5.6	101.2
41.0	4.0	County Road	5.4	101.0

From Vermont Line	Within Section		Within Section	From New York Line
North–South			**South–North**	
43.2	6.2	Finerty Pond	3.2	98.8
45.1	8.1	Becket Mountain (2,180')	1.3	96.9
45.6	8.6	Tyne Road	0.8	96.4
46.4	9.4	U.S. 20 (1,400')	0.0	95.6

Massachusetts Section Six

From Vermont Line	Within Section		Within Section	From New York Line
46.4	0.0	U.S. 20 (1,400')	8.6	95.6
46.7	0.3	Greenwater Brook	8.3	95.3
46.8	0.4	Massachusetts Turnpike (I-90)	8.2	95.2
48.0	1.6	Upper Goose Pond Cabin side trail	7.0	94.0
48.8	2.4	Upper Goose Pond	6.2	93.2
50.7	4.3	Goose Pond Road	4.3	91.3
53.1	6.7	Webster Road (1,800')	1.9	88.9
55.0	8.6	Tyringham Main Road (930')	0.0	87.0

Massachusetts Section Seven

From Vermont Line	Within Section		Within Section	From New York Line
55.0	0.0	Tyringham Main Road (930')	12.3	87.0
56.1	1.1	Jerusalem Road	11.2	85.9
58.1	3.1	Shaker Campsite side trail	9.2	83.9
58.4	3.4	Fernside Road	8.9	83.6
61.6	6.6	Beartown Mountain Road	5.7	80.4
62.2	7.2	Mt. Wilcox North Shelter side trail	5.1	79.8
64.0	9.0	Mt. Wilcox South Shelter side trail	3.3	78.0
64.7	9.7	The Ledges	2.6	77.3
65.3	10.3	Benedict Pond	2.0	76.7

North–South			**South–North**	
From Vermont Line	*Within Section*		*Within Section*	**From New York Line**
66.1	11.1	Blue Hill Road (Stony Brook Road)	1.2	75.9
67.3	12.3	Mass. 23 (1,000')	0.0	74.7

Massachusetts Section Eight

67.3	0.0	Mass. 23 (1,000')	8.4	74.7
68.2	0.9	Lake Buel Road	7.5	73.8
69.3	2.0	Tom Leonard Shelter side trail	6.4	72.7
71.4	4.1	East Mountain (1,800')	4.3	70.6
72.8	5.5	Homes Road	2.9	69.2
74.8	7.5	Housatonic River	0.9	67.2
75.7	8.4	U.S. 7	0.0	66.3

Massachusetts Section Nine

75.7	0.0	U.S. 7	4.5	66.3
77.5	1.8	South Egremont Road (700')	2.7	64.5
79.3	3.6	Mass. 41	0.9	62.7
80.2	4.5	Jug End Road (Curtiss Road)	0.0	61.8

Massachusetts Section Ten

80.2	0.0	Jug End Road (Curtiss Road)	9.5	61.8
81.3	1.1	Jug End (1,750')	8.4	60.7
83.0	2.8	Elbow Trail	6.7	59.0
83.6	3.4	Glen Brook Shelter side trail	6.1	58.4
83.7	3.5	Hemlocks Shelter side trail	6.0	58.3
84.1	3.9	Guilder Pond Picnic Area	5.6	57.9

North–South			South–North	
From Vermont Line	*Within Section*		*Within Section*	**From New York Line**
84.8	4.6	Mt. Everett (2,602')	4.9	57.2
85.5	5.3	Race Brook Falls Trail	4.2	56.5
86.6	6.4	Race Mountain	3.1	55.4
88.5	8.3	Laurel Ridge Campsite	1.2	53.5
89.7	9.5	Sages Ravine (1,340')	0.0	52.3

Connecticut Section One

89.7	0.0	Sages Ravine (1,340')	7.4	52.3
90.3	0.6	Sages Ravine Brook Campsite	6.8	51.7
90.4	0.7	Massachusetts–Connecticut Line	6.7	51.6
91.1	1.4	Bear Mountain (2,316')	6.0	50.9
91.8	2.1	Bear Mountain Road	5.3	50.2
92.0	2.3	Riga Junction, Undermountain Trail	5.1	50.0
92.5	2.8	Brassie Brook (South Branch), Brassie Brook Shelter	4.6	49.5
93.1	3.4	Ball Brook Campsite	4.0	48.9
93.7	4.0	Riga Shelter	3.4	48.3
94.4	4.7	Lions Head (1,738')	2.7	47.6
97.1	7.4	Conn. 41 (Undermountain Road)	0.0	44.9

Connecticut Section Two

97.1	0.0	Conn. 41 (Undermountain Road)	10.8	44.9
97.8	0.7	U.S. 44 (700')	10.1	44.2
100.3	3.2	Billy's View	7.6	41.7
101.1	4.0	Rand's View	6.8	40.9

North–South From Vermont Line	North–South Within Section		South–North Within Section	South–North From New York Line
101.2	4.1	Limestone Spring Shelter side trail	6.7	40.8
101.9	4.8	Prospect Mountain (1,475′)	6.0	40.1
104.7	7.6	Housatonic River Road	3.2	37.3
105.3	8.2	Iron Bridge over Housatonic River	2.6	36.7
107.2	10.1	Mohawk Trail	0.7	34.8
107.3	10.2	U.S. 7, Housatonic River (500′)	0.6	34.7
107.9	10.8	U.S. 7, Conn. 112	0.0	34.1

Connecticut Section Three

107.9	0.0	U.S. 7, Conn. 112	11.5	34.1
108.3	0.4	Belter's Campsite	11.1	33.7
111.1	3.2	Sharon Mountain Campsite	8.3	30.9
112.3	4.4	Mt. Easter (1,350′)	7.1	29.7
112.6	4.7	Sharon Mountain Road	6.8	29.4
113.5	5.6	Pine Swamp Brook Shelter side trail	5.9	28.5
114.6	6.7	West Cornwall Road (800′)	4.8	27.4
114.7	6.8	Carse Brook	4.7	27.3
116.9	9.0	Caesar Road, Caesar Brook Campsite	2.5	25.1
117.3	9.4	Pine Knob Loop Trail	2.1	24.7
118.0	10.1	Hatch Brook	1.4	24.0
119.2	11.3	Old Sharon Road	0.2	22.8
119.4	11.5	Conn. 4	0.0	22.6

North–South			**South–North**	
From Vermont Line	*Within Section*		*Within Section*	From New York Line
		Connecticut Section Four		
119.4	0.0	Conn. 4	11.1	22.6
120.3	0.9	Silver Hill Campsite side trail	10.2	21.7
121.1	1.7	River Road	9.4	20.9
123.1	3.7	Stony Brook campsites	7.4	18.9
123.5	4.1	Stewart Hollow Brook Shelter (400')	7.0	18.5
125.8	6.4	River Road	4.7	16.2
126.3	6.9	St. Johns Ledges	4.2	15.7
127.0	7.6	Caleb's Peak (1,160')	3.5	15.0
130.5	11.1	Conn. 341, Schaghticoke Road (350')	0.0	11.5
		Connecticut Section Five		
130.5	0.0	Conn. 341, Schaghticoke Road (350')	11.5	11.5
130.8	0.3	Mt. Algo Shelter side trail	11.2	11.2
131.8	1.3	Thayer Brook	10.2	10.2
133.7	3.2	Schaghticoke Mountain Campsite side trail	8.3	8.3
134.3	3.8	Indian Rocks	7.7	7.7
134.7	4.2	Connecticut–New York Line (1,250')	7.3	7.3
137.6	7.1	Schaghticoke Road	4.4	4.4
137.9	7.4	Bulls Bridge Road side trail	4.1	4.1
139.0	8.5	Ten Mile River (280')	3.0	3.0
139.2	8.7	Ten Mile River Shelter side trail	2.8	2.8
140.2	9.7	Ten Mile Hill (1,000')	1.8	1.8
141.3	10.8	Conn. 55	0.7	0.7
142.0	11.5	Hoyt Road, New York Line (400')	0.0	0.0

N

O

T

U

V

W

Acknowledgments

Primary contributors to this edition were Cosmo Catalano and Jim Pelletier for Massachusetts; and Ann Sherwood, Elaine LaBella, Dave Boone, Henry Edmonds, and Tom Evans for Connecticut.

This edition was built on the foundation of the longtime contributions of the previous editors, Norman Sills and Robert Hatton.

Sue Spring

Photography credits

1 Isaac Wiegmann; 4 Adam Daniel; 6 Bill Cooke, ATC; 7 Isaac Wiegmann (2); 42 Laurie Potteiger; 47 Laurie Potteiger; 57 Will Skinner; 59 Timothy Cummings; 69 Sally Naser; 83 Laurie Potteiger; 89 Isaac Wiegmann; 103 Bob Fletcher; 107 John Fletcher; 113 Bob Fletcher; 121 John Fletcher; 124 Bob Fletcher; 129 Chris Myers; 131 V. Collins Chew; 141 Chris Myers; 143 Michael Warren; 157 Bob Fletcher; 167 Isaac Wiegmann

For more information

Appalachian Trail Conservancy
ATC's central offices are located in Harpers Ferry, West Virginia. Membership services, program administration, and requests for information about the Trail are all handled there. The public Information Center is also located there. Regular business hours are 9 a.m.–5 p.m. ET, Monday–Friday, but the visitors center is open daily except Christmas and New Year's Day. Directions can be found on the Web site below. The mailing address and telephone numbers are:

Appalachian Trail Conservancy
P. O. Box 807
(799 Washington Street)
Harpers Ferry, WV 25425-0807
Telephone: (304) 535-6331
Fax: (304) 535-2667
<www.appalachiantrail.org>

Its New England office office is located at the Kellogg Conservation Center at the Trail crossing of Mass. 41 south of South Egremont, Mass. Mail: P.O. Box 264, South Egremont, MA 01258. Telephone: (413) 528-8002. E-mail: <atc-nero@appalachiantrail.org>

The Ultimate Appalachian Trail Store
The ATC sales distribution center is located in Kearneysville, West Virginia (179 East Burr Boulevard, Unit N, 25430). For customer service, call toll-free to (888) AT-STORE (888-287-8673) during weekday business hours (9 a.m.–4:30 p.m. ET) or e-mail <sales@appalachiantrail.org>.
Fax: (304) 724-8386
<www.atctrailstore.org>

Frequently Requested E-mail Addresses
Trail & hiking questions: <info@appalachiantrail.org>
ATC membership: <membership@appalachiantrail.org>
Merchandise: <sales@appalachiantrail.org>
Editor, *A.T. Journeys*: <editor@appalachiantrail.org>
Publisher, ATC books: <general@appalachiantrail.org>
Volunteer Trail crew program: <crews@appalachiantrail.org>
Reporting an incident: <incident@appalachiantrail.org>

You can help us protect and conserve the Appalachian Trail

Become a member of the
Appalachian Trail Conservancy at
www.appalachiantrail.org/join

Or by calling (304) 535-6331
Monday through Friday,
9 a.m. to 5 p.m. Eastern Time